From Your Friends At The MAILBOX®

NOVEMBER

A MONTH OF IDEAS AT YOUR FINGERTIPS!

GRADES 4–6

P9-BEE-721

WRITTEN BY
Becky Andrews, Irving P. Crump, Peggy W. Hambright,
Paula Holdren, Simone Lepine, Christine A. Thuman,
Lynn Tutterow, Patricia Twohey

EDITED BY
Becky Andrews, Lynn Bemer Coble,
Jennifer Rudisill, Gina Sutphin

ILLUSTRATED BY
Jennifer T. Bennett, Cathy Spangler Bruce, Pam Crane,
Teresa Davidson, Clevell Harris, Susan Hodnett, Sheila Krill,
Rebecca Saunders, Barry Slate, Donna Teal

COVER ART BY
Jennifer T. Bennett

www.themailbox.com

©1996 by THE EDUCATION CENTER, INC.
All rights reserved.
ISBN# 1-56234-129-4

Manufactured in the United States
10 9 8 7 6 5 4

TABLE OF CONTENTS

November Calendar 3
Highlight special November days with sensational activities.

November Planner Pages 5
Be prepared for a great month with these handy reproducibles.
Includes:
- A teacher's resource list of November's special days
- November clip art
- An open November newsletter to keep parents informed
- A reproducible calendar of free-time activities for students
- A reproducible award and a student desktag

Thumbs Up For Thanksgiving! 10
Celebrate the Thanksgiving season with a festive collection of fun
activities that gobble their way across the curriculum!

The Pilgrims Of Plymouth 18
Explore the impact this small group of colonists had on our nation
with exciting thematic activities and reproducibles.

Geography Gems 26
Chart your course for National Geography Awareness Week with an
assortment of fun ways to teach geography skills.

Setting The Stage For American Education Week 40
Honor your co-workers and explore the topic of schools with
thematic activities your young scholars will love.

Booking A Trip Around The World 54
Get ready for a first-class National Children's Book Week with
activities that guarantee an enthusiasm for reading.

Up, Up, And Away! 70
Explore aviation with hands-on activities that will send students
soaring to new learning heights.

The Road To The White House 80
Introduce students to the election process with stimulating activities
that are sure to win their vote of approval!

Heroes Of Freedom 90
Salute those who have fought for
freedom with thought-provoking
ideas for Veterans Day.

Answer Keys 95

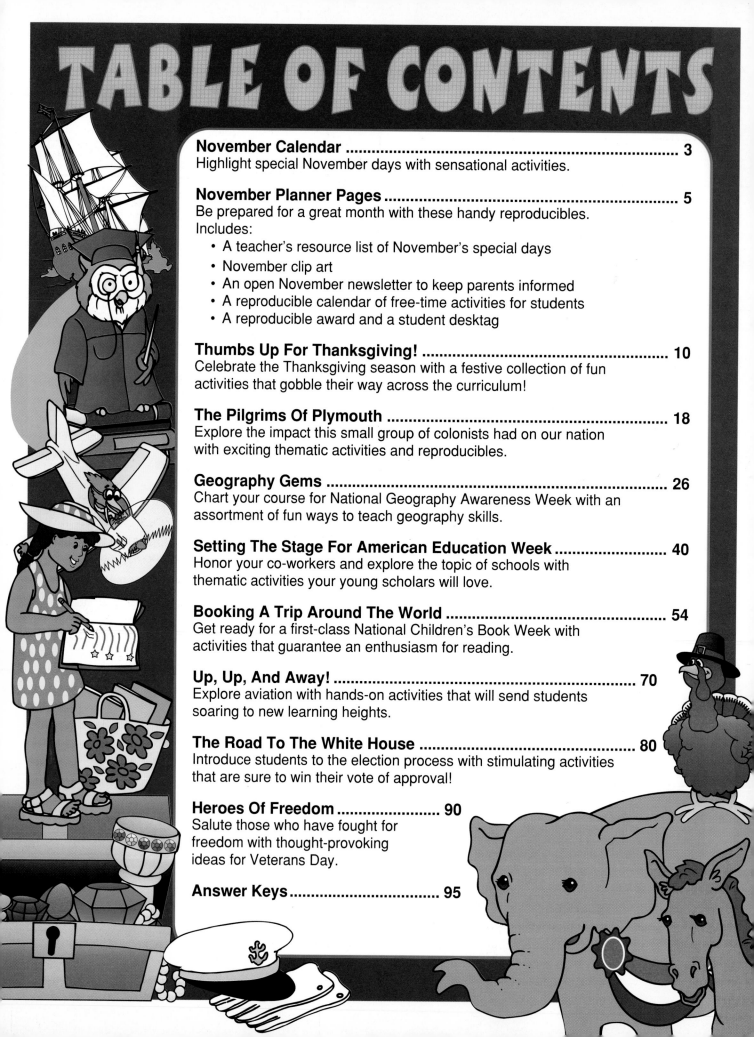

November Calendar

Peanut Butter Lovers' Month

In honor of the monthlong celebration of America's favorite food, have students invent ten new ways to eat peanut butter. Give each student a peanut-shaped cutout on which to write his thoughts. Post the peanut shapes around a student-made poster that shows the nutritive value of the peanut.

1—National Authors' Day

The purpose of National Authors' Day is to show appreciation to those who have made American literature possible. Write the names of favorite American authors suggested by students vertically on a chalkboard. Give each student a Post-It® Brand note on which to write her name. Direct each student to post her note on the chalkboard next to her favorite author's name. When everyone has voted, ask each student to illustrate the class data in a graph.

2—Daniel Boone's Birthday

As an American frontiersman, explorer, and militia officer, Daniel Boone led quite an adventurous life. Born on this day in 1734, Boone was once captured by Shawnee Indians and held captive for five months before escaping. During this time, he was adopted into the tribe as the chief's son. Ask each student to imagine what this experience must have been like for Daniel Boone. Then have the student write five questions he would have asked Daniel about his period of captivity.

3—Sandwich Day

John Montague, the Fourth Earl of Sandwich, was born on this day in 1718. He created the world's first fast food—the sandwich. Provide construction paper and other art materials. Ask each child to cut out shapes of bread and fillings for a sandwich. Have the student label each sandwich ingredient with a requirement for academic success, such as "Get plenty of rest," or "Use an assignment pad." Have the student staple the layers together at the top so that each ingredient can be read. Post the sandwiches on a board titled "Fast Food For Academic Success."

4—Opening Of The Erie Canal

The Erie Canal, the first major waterway built in the United States, opened on this date in 1825. It stretched across northern New York State and linked the eastern seaboard with the Great Lakes. Share the Erie Canal portion of *The Story Of America's Canals* by Ray Spangenburg and Diane Moser (Facts On File, 1992) with your students. Then have them locate the Erie Canal on a map and pen the lyrics to a song that workers on the canal could have sung while working.

(Turn the page for more…)

12—Birthday Of François Auguste Rodin

The great French sculptor who got everybody thinkin' was born on this day in 1840. Rodin gave the world many great sculptured pieces of art, but one of his most famous works is *The Thinker.* Show students a picture of this sculpture from an encyclopedia or other resource. Then ask each student to ponder what the man in the sculpture is thinking, elaborate on it in a descriptive paragraph, and then share her paragraph with the class.

15—American Enterprise Day

American Enterprise Day is sponsored by the Future Business Leaders of America as a special day to celebrate the achievements of American business and industry. Discuss with students the changes that have taken place in the business arena due to a changing world. Ask students how new inventions, mass production, computers, faster transportation, and speedier communication systems have affected the number and types of products available today. Then have each student write a paragraph describing a future need that the American public might have and a product that could be produced to meet that need.

21—World Hello Day

The purpose of World Hello Day is to advance peace through personal communication. Use *Who Talks Funny? A Book About Languages For Kids* by Brenda S. Cox (Linnet Books, 1995) to research ways of saying hello in different languages. Share these with your students. Challenge each student to learn as many ways of saying hello as he can. Have the students say hello in a different language to at least ten other people during the day.

Shalom   Bonjour   Hola
Ciao   Hello   Guten Tag
Moshi moshi

22—National Stop The Violence Day

National Stop The Violence Day is observed on the anniversary of President John F. Kennedy's assassination. Since 1990, radio and television stations have used this day to promote "peace on the streets" and an end to violence. Have groups of students suggest ways to curb the growing problem of violence and offer solutions for a safer future. Allow time for each group to share and discuss its suggestions with the class.

National Game And Puzzle Week

Games and puzzles of every type and description imaginable are the focus of National Game and Puzzle Week. Observed annually the last week of November, the week's purpose is to increase appreciation of games and puzzles while promoting time spent with family and friends. Ask each student to describe in a paragraph the game or puzzle he most likes to enjoy with a family member and why he likes it. Then allow the student to bring that favorite game or puzzle to school to share with a friend during free time.

Teacher's November Resource Calendar
A Handy List Of Special Days

The early Roman calendar began with March, so November was its ninth month. *Novem* is the Latin word for "nine."

1 The first plastic hockey mask was invented on this day in 1959 by Montreal Canadiens goalie Jacques Plante.

2 The *Hercules*—later nicknamed the "Spruce Goose"—made its only flight on this date in 1947. This huge, flying boat was designed, built, and flown by millionaire Howard Hughes.

6 James Naismith, the inventor of the game of basketball, was born on this day in 1861.

7 The Canadian Pacific's Transcontinental Railway was completed on this date in 1885.

8 Edmund Halley—the man who observed and accurately predicted the return of the comet later named for him—was born on this day in 1656.

9 On this date in 1906, President Theodore Roosevelt became the first president to travel outside the country while still in office when he sailed to the Panama Canal Zone.

10 On this day in 1871, explorer Henry M. Stanley found David Livingstone, an explorer-missionary who'd been missing for two years in Africa.

12 William "Pudge" Heffelfinger became the first professional football player on this day in 1892 when he received a $500 cash bonus for playing in a football game.

14 The inventor of the steamboat, Robert Fulton, was born on this day in 1765.

17 The Suez Canal was formally opened on this date in 1869.

21 U.S. Army surgeon William Beaumont was born on this day in 1785. He observed the stomach and digestive processes through a shotgun wound in a fur trapper's abdomen and later published his findings.

25 Andrew Carnegie—a wealthy American philanthropist whose gifts include Carnegie Hall, the Carnegie Foundation, and more than 2,500 libraries—was born on this day in 1835.

30 Samuel Langhorne Clemens (Mark Twain)—the author of *The Adventures Of Tom Sawyer, The Adventures Of Huckleberry Finn,* and *The Prince And The Pauper*—was born on this day in 1835.

November Clip Art

Use on the following items:

- letters to parents
- games
- nametags
- notes to students
- homework assignments
- newsletters
- awards
- learning centers
- bulletin boards

CLASSROOM TIMES

Teacher: _____ Date: _____

NOVEMBER

Special Events

Hats Off To...

Help Wanted

Highlights

Don't Forget

FREE-TIME FUN for November!

Tackle these 20 terrific tasks when you finish your work.

Monday	Tuesday	Wednesday	Thursday	Friday
Eight letters spell *November.* List eight-letter words associated with this month. (Ex. *thankful*)	Describe five ways you could use fallen leaves.	Invent a new musical instrument. Describe the sound it makes and how it is played.	Use the words *pin* and *pen* correctly in the same sentence. *pin pen*	Write an emergency plan for your family in case your home is ever without electricity.
Use the word *cook* twice in the same sentence—once as a noun and again as a verb. *cook cook*	Suggest three ways to get more people out to the polls to vote during elections.	Write a riddle about your favorite holiday.	Estimate how long it takes you to write your full name. Then time yourself to see how long it takes.	Without a ruler, draw a line about seven inches long. Then measure to see how accurate you are.
Use the letters in *November* to write as many different words as you can. *November*	Estimate how many cups of water it would take to fill a two-liter bottle. Then measure to find out.	National Clean Out Your Refrigerator Day is November 20. What other things have to be cleaned out frequently?	List ten things you are thankful for. Explain why you are thankful for each one.	Plan a Thanksgiving Day meal for your family. Tell in which food group each menu item belongs.
What meats will your classmates who don't like turkey eat on Thanksgiving Day? Find out; then graph the data.	Make a list of ten things that can be done with a cooked turkey besides eating it.	Your five-year-old cousin is getting the wishbone *you* want at this year's Thanksgiving Day dinner. Write your reaction.	Listen carefully and identify ten different sounds going on around you right now.	Show what your name would look like if you were to read it from paper held in front of a mirror. JA AL

8

Note To The Teacher: Have each student staple a copy of this page inside a file folder. Direct students to store their completed work inside their folders.

Desktag: Duplicate student copies on construction paper. Have each student personalize and decorate his pattern; then laminate the patterns and use them as desktags during November.

Award: Duplicate multiple copies. Keep them handy at your desk during the month of November. When a student earns an award, write the assignment for which she is being rewarded on the appropriate line. Provide scissors and crayons or markers for the student to use in completing the bookmark.

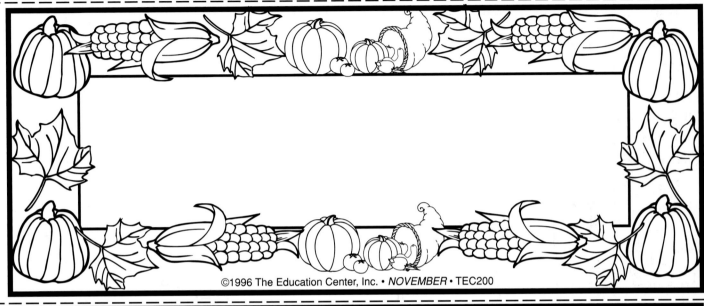

©1996 The Education Center, Inc. • *NOVEMBER* • TEC200

Date: _____

From: _____

Hats Off To

_____
(name of student)

for doing a gobblin' great job on

_____
(assignment)

Cut out and color the bookmark below. Use it while you enjoy ten extra minutes of free time reading your favorite book.

©1996 The Education Center, Inc. • *NOVEMBER* • TEC200

What A Gobblin' Great Book!

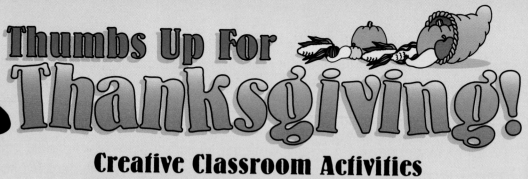

Thumbs Up For Thanksgiving!

Creative Classroom Activities For Celebrating "Turkey Day"

Sitting down to enjoy a Thanksgiving meal with family and friends—it's one of the oldest customs on Earth. Celebrate the spirit and simplicity of Thanksgiving with the following creative teaching activities.

by Irving P. Crump and Lynn Tutterow

Before The Pilgrims

Ask any intermediate student to describe the first Thanksgiving and he or she will probably relate the story of the Pilgrims' harsh first year in the New World—and the feast we call the "first" Thanksgiving. But Thanksgiving's roots extend to biblical times. Moses, the leader of the Hebrews, told his people how to celebrate the Feast of the Tabernacles, a celebration much like our Thanksgiving. The ancient Greeks also held thanksgiving celebrations every year after a good harvest.

But for Americans, Thanksgiving commemorates a small group of colonists who journeyed across the Atlantic so they could worship as they pleased. It is a time to give thanks not only for nature's bounty, but also for freedom. Read aloud the First Amendment to the Constitution. Ask students what these basic freedoms mean and why they were so important to our founding fathers. Have students share their thoughts about this amendment in essays titled "The First Amendment: What It Means To Me." Let students copy their essays on copies of the pattern on page 22.

Thank-You Board

Watch this appealing display fill up quickly with tons of thank-yous! Cover a classroom or hallway bulletin board with white paper. Add the title "Thank You!" near the top of the display. Provide a supply of colorful markers and crayons nearby. Get the ball rolling by writing (directly on the paper) the name of someone you wish to thank for a kind deed. Add a comma after the person's name; then express your thankfulness in a brief sentence. Invite other faculty members and students to add to this gigantic thank-you card.

THANK YOU!

Mrs. Wilson,
Thanks for helping me with my multiplication facts.

Danny

A Land Of Plenty

What are your students most thankful for when they think about living in America? Give them an opportunity to share their thoughts through this simple art activity. Provide each small group of students with a large sheet of white construction paper. Have each group draw an outline of the United States on the paper and cut it out. Then instruct each group to cut pictures that depict things for which they are thankful—particularly things about living in "the land of the free"—from old magazines, to glue collage-fashion inside the U.S. outline. Display the completed projects along a hallway near your classroom with the title "This Land Of Plenty."

Thankful Through The Years

For a unique Thanksgiving project, give each student 10–12 large, unlined index cards. Have the student fold each card in half, then unfold it. Across the top of a card, instruct the student to write "When I was one year old,…." Have him write "When I was two years old,…" on the second card and continue labeling the cards up to his current age. Have each student take his cards home. With parental assistance, have the student describe and illustrate a positive event that occurred to him or his family during that year of his life on the left side of each card. The next day provide references to help students locate a positive historical event that occurred during each year of their lives. Have students describe and illustrate these events on the right sides of their cards. When the cards are completed, have each student punch a hole in the top left-hand corner of each one and tie the cards together (in order) with yarn, adding a cover titled "Thankful Through The Years." Encourage students to continue adding cards to these keepsake booklets during the upcoming years.

"Turkey Day" Greeting Cards

Turn your classroom into a greeting card factory with this perfect-for-a-Friday-afternoon activity! Duplicate page 17 for each student. In addition, provide each student with a sheet of duplicating paper. Instruct students to fold their sheets into three sections, then unfold them. Direct students to copy or trace the various borders, characters, and letters on the reproducible to create cards for their parents or other special relatives or friends. Have students decorate their cards with colored pencils or markers. When the cards are completed, provide students with business-size envelopes in which to mail their greetings.

An Easy Bulletin Board? Thanks!

Need a simple bulletin board for the Thanksgiving season? Also need some good writing topics for November? Look no more! Duplicate a copy of the writing activities on page 16 for each student. While students are working on their writings, cut letters to spell "THANKS!" out of large pieces of yellow bulletin-board paper or poster board. After each child has written his final copy for each topic he chose and mounted it on a piece of construction paper, divide the class into six groups. Give each group one of the letter cutouts (including the exclamation mark). Have the group color the letter with designs using colorful markers. Post the letters in the middle of a bulletin board; then arrange the students' written work around the letters. Now, thankfully, wasn't that simple? *(For another simple November bulletin board, see "Thank-You Board" on page 10.)*

'Twas The Night Before Thanksgiving...

...And all through your classroom, you'll hear giggles of creative glee with this fun project! Share with students Clement Clarke Moore's famous poem, " 'Twas The Night Before Christmas." Then divide the class into groups and provide each group with a copy of the ballad. Instruct each group to write a new (and shorter) version of the poem titled " 'Twas The Night Before Thanksgiving." Have the groups write their ballads from a turkey's point of view.

Tabletop Turkeys

Create colorful turkey napkin rings to add a festive touch to students' Thanksgiving mealtimes. Begin by collecting enough empty toilet-tissue tubes so that each student has one. Then provide each student with a copy of page 14 (duplicated on tagboard or other sturdy paper if possible), plus a half-sheet (9" x 6") each of red, yellow, orange, and brown construction paper and the other materials listed on page 14. The reproducible gives directions for making one napkin ring. Suggest that each student make at least two to four napkin rings for her Thanksgiving table. Since four turkey bodies can be cut from each toilet-tissue tube, one tube per student will be sufficient.

Bird, Beast, Or Fish?

What was it like being on board the *Mayflower* for 66 long (and probably very boring!) days? Share with students that the children on the ship were not allowed on deck, so there was no room for playing games or running around. To pass the time, they studied their lessons and played quiet games. In one such game, a leader pointed to a player and said, "Bird," "Beast," or "Fish." That player then had to respond with an animal name that matched the category before the leader counted to ten. An animal name could not be repeated. If a player couldn't think of one within ten seconds, he lost and was out of the game. The game grew more difficult as the more common animal names were used.

Play a similar game as a five-minute filler during the Thanksgiving season. Use categories related to topics you're currently studying (for example: "State, state capital, or Canadian province"; "Multiple of 2, multiple of 5, or multiple of 7"; etc.).

Share The Spirit

Looking over a delicious, bountiful Thanksgiving spread reminds us not only of how thankful we are, but also that there are many people who are not as fortunate. Use this theme of sharing to motivate your class or grade level to sponsor a schoolwide canned food drive. Plan to begin the drive about two or three weeks before Thanksgiving to allow plenty of time to divvy up responsibilities to students. Be sure to let students make as many decisions as possible about the drive, with you acting as a facilitator. As canned foods come into your classroom, provide students with more copies of page 17. Have students use colorful construction-paper strips and the graphics on that page to create bands of Thanksgiving greetings to wrap around the tops of the cans.

Tabletop Turkey

Add a festive touch to your family's Thanksgiving meal with this colorful turkey napkin ring!

Materials: red, yellow, orange, and brown construction paper; ruler; pencil; scissors; glue; toilet-tissue tube; black, felt-tipped marker

Make the tail:

1. Carefully cut out the eight patterns on the left side of this page.
2. Following the directions on each one, trace the patterns on construction paper. You will make 14 strips in all.
3. Cut out each colored strip.
4. Loop each feather strip over without creasing it. Glue the ends together as shown. Set it aside to dry.
5. Lightly draw a line on the brown body strip, 1/4 inch from the top (as shown on the pattern). Also make a light mark in the middle of this strip where indicated on the pattern. Place the body strip in front of you with the pencil lines showing.
6. Glue the two long orange loops onto the body strip—one on either side of the midpoint pencil mark. The bottom edges of the orange loops should touch the horizontal pencil line. Hold each loop in place a little while to dry.
7. Next glue two long yellow loops, two red loops, two brown loops, two short orange loops, and two short yellow loops—in the order shown.

glue

orange
yellow
red
brown
orange
yellow
yellow
red
brown
orange
yellow
midpoint

Make the head:

1. Curl one end of the head strip around your finger to make a loop. Glue the loop in place as shown.
2. Add details by cutting pieces of construction paper and gluing them on the head. Use the marker to draw eyes.
3. Measure about 1/2 inch from the other end of the head strip and make a pencil mark. Fold back this end to make a tab.

glue

glue

Complete the project:

1. Measure about 1 inch from one end of the toilet-tissue tube, make a mark, and cut off this section. This is the turkey's body.
2. With its penciled side up, apply a thin layer of glue along the feather strip. Wrap it around the tube, overlapping a little. Hold it in place until the glue dries.
3. Bend the feathers up to look like a turkey's tail.
4. Apply glue to the tab at the bottom of the head as shown. Attach it to the body. Hold it in place until the glue dries.

Feathers: Make 2 brown tracings.

Feathers: Make 2 orange tracings.

Feathers: Make 2 yellow tracings.

Feathers: Make 2 yellow tracings.

Feathers: Make 2 red tracings.

1/4 inch

Make 1 brown tracing for the body.

midpoint

Make 1 brown tracing for the head.

Feathers: Make 2 orange tracings.

Name_____ *Math, using a calculator*

Cashing In With Coupons

Coupons can add up to great savings. Before heading to the checkout counter, check out the savings on the coupons featured on this page. Use the information on the coupons and a calculator to fill in each blank in the Thanksgiving shopping list below. **Hint:** Double-check your work. The total cost of the grocery items minus the total savings of the coupons should equal the total bill. Also: not all of the coupons will be used.

Thanksgiving Shopping List

item	cost without coupon	value of coupon	cost after using coupon
8 lb. turkey	$1.09/lb. = _____	_____	_____
16-oz. can pumpkin-pie filling	$0.08/oz. = _____	_____	_____
2 gal. milk	$2.29/gal. = _____	_____	_____
2 doz. eggs	$1.49/doz. = _____	_____	_____
1 doz. ears of corn	$0.09/ear = _____	_____	_____
1 pkg. of 2 pie shells	$1.25/pkg. = _____	_____	_____
8 lbs. potatoes	$0.49/lb. = _____	_____	_____
1 pkg. rolls	$1.39/pkg. = _____	_____	_____
2 pkg. stuffing mix	$0.98/pkg. = _____	_____	_____
15 large tea bags	$0.79/box of 5 = _____	_____	_____
	total cost before coupons =	**total savings with coupons =**	**total bill =**

Coupons (left side):

POTATOES 5¢ OFF PER POUND COUPON

COUPON — Buy 1 Doz. Ears Get 2 Free! EXPIRES 2/96

½ BUY ONE DOZEN SECOND DOZEN ½ OFF! ½ COUPON

COUPON — 20¢ OFF ANY PIE FILLING

35¢ OFF! PKG. OF 2 PIE SHELLS COUPON

Coupons (right side):

BESTEA 10¢ OFF PER BOX WHEN PURCHASING 2 OR MORE COUPON

COUPON — ALL TURKEYS 10¢ OFF PRICE PER POUND

30¢ OFF Stuffing Mix 2 or more COUPON

COUPON — 50¢ OFF! MILK EXPIRES 1/96

COUPON — SAVE! 20¢ PER PACKAGE Bakery-Fresh Rolls

Bonus Box: Calculate the tax on your total grocery bill. Use a 6% rate, or 0.06, and round to the nearest cent. What would your total be after tax is added?

Thank You! Thank You! Thank You!

Thank you very much! I appreciate what you did! I'm very grateful! Thanks a lot! No matter how you say it, telling someone "thank you"—for whatever reason—is simply good manners and takes little time or effort.

Read the topics below. Choose three to write about. When you're finished, have a friend proofread each completed writing for you. Then rewrite all three in your very best cursive handwriting, each on a separate sheet of paper.

And...thank you!

- Did Grandma send you a crisp $10 bill on your last birthday? Or perhaps Uncle Pete gave you the latest R. L. Stine book. Did you, by chance, forget to write a thank-you note? (It happens!) But it's never too late to express thanks to someone. Write a thank-you note to someone who's given you a gift in the recent past, and whom you've forgotten to thank properly. Begin with an apology for taking so long to write.

- Is there a special coach, Sunday school teacher, scout leader, or other adult in your life whom you really look up to? Write that person a thank-you letter, describing why you appreciate him or her.

- What famous person would you like to say "thank you" to? An inventor? An entertainer? A sports hero? Write a letter to that person that includes several reasons why you are thanking him or her.

- When accepting special awards, entertainers are sometimes completely surprised and have a difficult time expressing their thanks. Others prepare their acceptance speeches ahead of time—just in case they win! What special award would you like to win? Write a brief acceptance speech that expresses your gratitude.

- Have you ever been thankful for something...but then later changed your mind? Write about this experience.

- Have you ever seen a "Thank You For Not Smoking" sign? In what places would you like to see similar signs? Perhaps a "Thank You For Not Littering" sign on your street? Make a list (or draw pictures) of five "Thank You For Not..." signs you would love to see.

Note To The Teacher: Use with "An Easy Bulletin Board? Thanks!" on page 12.

ABCDEFGHIJKLM
NOPQRSTUVWXYZ

We Give Thanks

Note To The Teacher: See "'Turkey Day' Greeting Cards" on page 11 and "Share The Spirit" on page 13 for suggestions on using this page of graphics.

The Pilgrims Of Plymouth

From the difficult journey across the Atlantic aboard the tiny *Mayflower*, to the encounters with Native Americans, to the joy of the first Thanksgiving feast, the story of the Pilgrims is one of courage and determination. Use the following creative teaching ideas and reproducibles to share this beginning chapter of American history with your students.

by Lynn Tutterow and Irving P. Crump

Cramped Quarters

On September 16, 1620, a group of 102 settlers set sail across the Atlantic Ocean on the *Mayflower*. The *Mayflower's* sister ship, the *Speedwell,* had proved to be unseaworthy and was abandoned in Southampton, England. Thus the *Mayflower*—overcrowded with its 44 *Saints* (Pilgrims) and 58 *Strangers* (other colonists) set sail alone.

Just how crowded were the conditions aboard the *Mayflower?* Each person's sleeping area was approximately six feet by three feet. To simulate this amount of space, push three desks together at the front of your classroom. Ask a volunteer to sit on the desks. Next give this student his books, bookbag, and other belongings to store in his "bunk" space. Continue handing items to the student until they topple onto the floor. Remind students that on the *Mayflower,* things were crammed to the ceilings! Everyone had brought possessions to last a lifetime in the New World. And amid these items, the Pilgrims also prepared their meals, ate, slept, washed, and passed the long hours of their 66-day voyage. After this demonstration, have each student list the ten items he would be sure to take with him on a trip to live in a new land. Have students write their lists on copies of the reproducible on page 22.

The Tiny *Mayflower*

The *Mayflower* probably looked like most other ships of its time, which generally had three masts and two decks. It measured about 90 feet from stem to stern, and was about 25 feet across at its widest point. It weighed about 180 short tons.

Send two student volunteers outside to a play area to create an approximate outline of the *Mayflower*. Provide the pair with a large ball of string and two yardsticks. Instruct the two students to measure and then lay string on the ground in a 90' x 25' rectangle. When the outline is complete, take the rest of the class to the area and have students step inside the outline to get a better feel of the actual size of the *Mayflower*. Invite two or three other classes to join your students to more accurately reflect the number of passengers (102) on board the *Mayflower.*

Plymouth Rock Poems

Rock Of Freedom

Plymouth Rock is a huge granite boulder with the date 1620 carved on it. It lies under a granite canopy near the place where the Pilgrims are believed to have first set foot when they landed in America. Bring a rock to class and paint the year 1620 on it. Show it to students; then lead a discussion about the Pilgrims and their struggle for religious freedom. Why did the Pilgrims have such a "rocky" start in the New World? Who was the "rock" on the voyage across the Atlantic to America? Who was the "rock" who helped save the Pilgrims during the first harsh winter? Next instruct each student to compose a poem about Plymouth Rock and the desire for freedom that it symbolizes. Have each student write the final draft of her poem on a piece of gray or brown construction paper that she has torn into a rock shape. Staple the paper rocks around a large, gray Plymouth Rock on a bulletin board as shown. Add the title "Plymouth Rock Poems."

The Importance Of Salt

Show students a container of salt and ask them to list ways salt is used. They'll likely respond that salt improves the taste of many foods. But what happens when we eat heavily salted foods? Serve your students a salty snack such as popcorn, party mix, or pretzels. How long is it before students are thirsty? Next provide students with some warm root beer or *Swizzle,* a cooling drink consumed by the Pilgrims (see the recipe on page 21). Ask students if their thirst has been quenched. Explain that because of salty diets, passengers on the *Mayflower* often needed to drink fluids.

The Legend Of The Five Kernels

Food was scarce during the Pilgrims' first winter in the New World. Governor John Carver gave each person five kernels of Indian corn once a day. When spring came, the Pilgrims planted some of this corn. The Pilgrims knew they would never face starvation again. From then on, they placed five kernels of corn on each person's plate when there was a time of thanksgiving.

Instruct each student to list five good things in his life for which he is thankful on a large index card. Provide each student with a five-inch square of cellophane, an eight-inch piece of yarn, and five kernels of candy corn. After placing his candy corn kernels in the center of the cellophane, have each student bundle them up into a bag and tie it off with yarn. Have students take their writings and bags of corn home to share with their families.

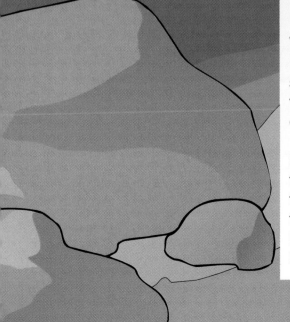

T Is For...

Have students tell the Pilgrim story with these creative projects. Have each student accordion-fold a 4" x 24" piece of white paper into 12 two-inch sections as shown. Next have the student spell *Thanksgiving* on the paper—one letter per section. Then have students write and illustrate an acrostic line for each letter in *Thanksgiving.* Display the completed cards on a table or on top of a bookcase.

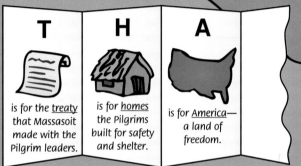

T is for the <u>treaty</u> that Massasoit made with the Pilgrim leaders.

H is for <u>homes</u> the Pilgrims built for safety and shelter.

A is for <u>America</u>— a land of freedom.

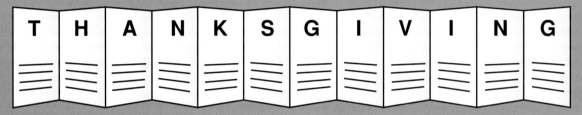

Pilgrim Papers

Use the reproducible parchment paper on page 22 and the bulletin-board characters and writing suggestions on page 23 to create a display of students' writings. First enlarge the Pilgrim boy and girl on the top half of page 23. Have student volunteers color the characters for you, then attach the characters to the center of a board titled "Pilgrim Papers." Duplicate one copy of the pattern on page 22 and one copy of the topics on the bottom of page 23 for each student. Have each student choose a topic to write about. Instruct each child to copy his final onto his sheet of parchment, adding an illustration at the top. Mount the pages on the bulletin board.

Indentured Servants

Divide students into pairs and give each pair a sheet of white construction paper. Have each pair of students work together and copy *only* the following on its sheet:

Four Freedoms
Freedom of speech and expression
Freedom to worship in your own way
Freedom from want
Freedom from fear

After each pair has finished its writing, take up all of the sheets. Tear each one in half and give a half-sheet back to each student. Next have students quietly circulate around the classroom to find the matching halves of their pieces of paper.

After students have found their matches, explain that among the *Mayflower's* 102 passengers were 18 servants. These servants were *indentured,* or bound, to their Pilgrim owners for seven years. An early *indenture* was a kind of special parchment contract. When it was ripped into two equal halves, the edges became ragged, or "indented." Each party kept one half. Then, if any disagreement arose concerning the contract, questions would be settled by matching the jagged edges of the two halves.

Swizzle

Ingredients: 1 quart water, 3/4 cup molasses, 1/4 cup white vinegar, 1/2 teaspoon ginger

To make: Mix all of the ingredients in a glass jar. Put a lid on the jar and shake it well. Refrigerate overnight and serve cold. Let each student take a small sip.

Bannock Cakes

Ingredients: 1 cup water, 1 cup stone-ground corn-meal, 1/2 teaspoon salt, 1/2 cup milk, 1 egg, 2 table-spoons butter

To make: Bring the cup of water to a boil. Mix the corn-meal and salt with a fork. Add the boiling water to the mixture. Stir until it is smooth. Then stir in the milk. Let the batter sit for about five minutes; then beat in the egg. Melt two tablespoons of butter in a heavy frying pan over medium heat. Drop the batter from a table-spoon to make little, round cakes. Cook the cakes for about two minutes. Turn each cake with a spatula and cook the other side for about one minute. Place the finished cakes on a serving dish. Serve either hot or cold. Makes approximately 25 four-inch cakes.

Pilgrim Recipes

Although the Pilgrims came to America more than 150 years before our nation became an independent country, we have learned a lot about them by reading their letters and diaries and by examining the pictures they drew. We can also eat the foods that they ate. On the left are two Pilgrim recipes: one for a drink called Swizzle and one for Bannock Cakes. Share these recipes with your students to try at home. Invite students to bring their completed creations to class and have a tasting party. Or have parent volunteers help you make them in class.

Day-To-Day Life

The daily lives of the Pilgrims were very different from life today. For example, meal-times were not a time for socializing. Children usually did not even sit at the table; they stood by their parents. No one had his or her own plate. Instead, two people would share a plate called a *trencher,* a bowl carved out of a block of wood. And many Pilgrims didn't even have these items. They used pieces of stale bread as plates.

These and scores of other interesting facts about the Pilgrims are presented in Lucille Recht Penner's book *Eating The Plates: A Pilgrim Book Of Food And Manners* (Macmillan Publishing Company). For other excellent resources students can use to learn about the Pilgrims, try these:
- *The First Thanksgiving* by Jean Craighead George (Philomel Books)
- *N. C. Wyeth's Pilgrims* by Robert San Souci (Chronicle)
- *Homes In The Wilderness: A Pilgrim's Journal Of Plymouth Plantation In 1629* by William Bradford et al.; edited by Margaret Wise Brown (Linnet Books)
- *Pilgrim Voices: Our First Year In The New World* edited by Connie and Peter Roop (Walker Publishing Company, Inc.)

Pattern

See "Cramped Quarters" on page 18 and "Pilgrim Papers" on page 20 for suggestions on using this pattern.

Name

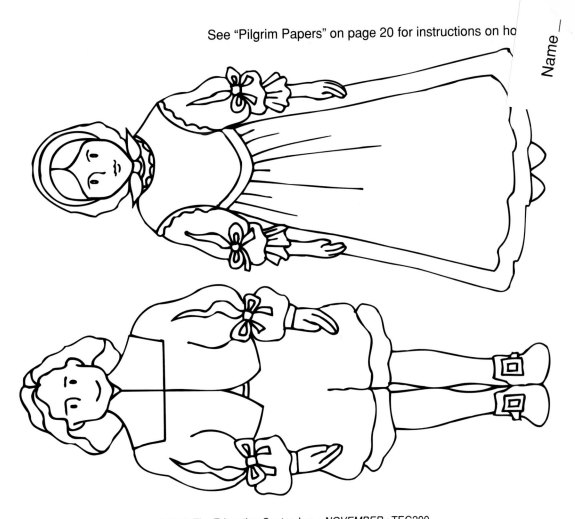

©1996 The Education Center, Inc. • *NOVEMBER* • TEC200

- -

Name _____ *Writing topics*

"...Doubt Nothing Of Its Truth"

...is what one Pilgrim said about the story he wrote. Choose one of the following writing topics. After you've completed a rough draft, give it to a classmate to edit. Then write your final copy on the piece of parchment provided by your teacher.

Descriptive Paragraph:
Describe the *Mayflower.* What kind of ship was she? How many decks? Tell about her size. Why was she so overcrowded? What problems did the ship have crossing the Atlantic? How and where was food stored on the ship? What about other supplies?

Informative Paragraph:
Tell about the hardships the Pilgrims faced during their voyage across the Atlantic. Be sure that your paragraph includes all facts.

Persuasive Paragraph:
Some Pilgrims left their children behind, promising to send for them when the settlement in the New World was off to a good start. Pretend you are a nine- or ten-year-old whose parents are planning for the voyage to America—but are leaving you behind. Write a one-paragraph letter to your parents persuading them to let you go on the voyage too.

©1996 The Education Center, Inc. • *NOVEMBER* • TEC200

New World Words

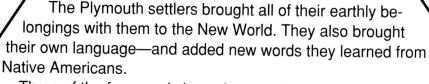

spices

herbs

The Plymouth settlers brought all of their earthly be-longings with them to the New World. They also brought their own language—and added new words they learned from Native Americans.

Three of the four words in each group below belong together. Mark out the word that does not belong with the other three. Then choose a category shown on this page and write it in the blank. On the back, write a sentence telling why each marked-out word does not belong in the category.

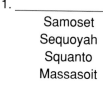
Plymouth craftsmen

seekers of religious freedom

1. _____
   Samoset
   Sequoyah
   Squanto
   Massasoit

2. _____
   eels
   kelp
   clams
   mussels

3. _____
   croutons
   wild onions
   leeks
   watercress

4. _____
   parsley
   sage
   marjoram
   tomatoes

5. _____
   settles
   trundle beds
   ottomans
   tables

6. _____
   cabbage
   carrots
   sweet potatoes
   turnips

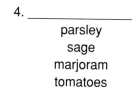
Plymouth leaders

ships of the 1620s

7. _____
   sawyers
   tanners
   printers
   coopers

8. _____
   cinnamon
   ginger
   abalone
   cloves

9. _____
   Mayflower
   Speedwell
   Fortune
   Godspeed

10. _____
    John Carver
    William Bradford
    Peregrine White
    Christopher Jones

11. _____
    Cape Cod Bay
    Hudson Bay
    Narragansett Bay
    Buzzards Bay

12. _____
    Saints
    Separatists
    Pilgrims
    Strangers

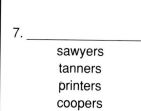

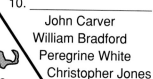
Massachusetts bodies of water

root vegetables

sea animals used for food

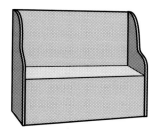
Pilgrim furniture

plants used in a Pilgrim salad

Indians the Pilgrims met

Plymouth: Ten Years Later

Plymouth Colony was founded in 1620 by a small band of Pilgrims who sailed from England aboard the *Mayflower*. They sailed around the tip of Cape Cod and first landed at Provincetown on November 21, 1620. The Pilgrims later sailed around Cape Cod Bay to Plymouth, settling there on December 26, 1620.

The map below shows Plymouth Colony in 1630—ten years after the arrival of the Pilgrims.

Label the map with the following terms. Use the clues below and other facts on this page to help you.

- Provincetown
- Cape Cod
- Cape Cod Bay
- Plymouth
- Massachusetts Bay Colony
- Boston
- Martha's Vineyard
- Nantucket
- Eastham
- Duxbury
- Providence
- Buzzards Bay
- Narragansett Bay
- North Atlantic Ocean
- Rehoboth
- Marshfield
- Rhode Island

Clues:

- The Massachusetts Bay Colony is northwest of Plymouth Colony.
- Boston is a Massachusetts port.
- Rehoboth is a settlement in the western part of Plymouth Colony.
- Duxbury is across Plymouth Bay from Plymouth.
- Martha's Vineyard is a large island south of Plymouth Colony.
- Nantucket is an island southeast of Martha's Vineyard.
- Rhode Island is west of Plymouth Colony.
- Providence was founded in eastern Rhode Island in 1636.
- Narragansett Bay borders both Plymouth Colony and Rhode Island.
- The settlement of Eastham is on the ocean side of Cape Cod.
- Marshfield is about four miles northwest of Duxbury.
- A string of islands separates Buzzards Bay from the Atlantic Ocean.

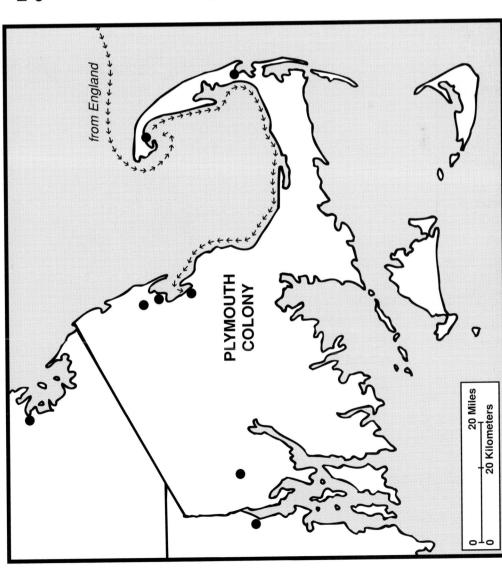

from England

PLYMOUTH COLONY

20 Miles

20 Kilometers

Geography Gems

Creative Activities To Improve Geography Skills

Tired of digging in your files for a fresh, new way to sharpen geography skills? Then take a closer look at this treasure trove of geography activities—perfect for National Geography Awareness Week (usually the third full week in November) or anytime you want to improve students' geographical know-how.

by Patricia Twohey

Travel six steps north. Take four steps northeast. Turn to the east.

Take two steps toward the pencil sharpener. Go straight past the third desk. Stop near the math center.

X Marks The Spot!

Keep your students on their directional toes with this fun location game. Mount posters labeled with the *cardinal directions* (north, south, east, and west) on appropriate walls in your classroom or gym. Review *absolute directions* (north, southeast, west, etc.) and *relative directions* (near, next to, etc.) with students.

Begin by choosing one student to be the *Locator*. Instruct the Locator to turn around and hide her eyes while the rest of the class scatters around the playing area. Call out, "Freeze location!" Each student should stop moving and remain in one spot. Silently select a student to be *Student X* and another student to be the *Navigator*. Direct the Navigator to give directions to the Locator as to the identity/location of Student X, without using student names or giving feedback about the correctness of the Locator's movements. Instruct the Locator to follow the Navigator's directions until she thinks she has located Student X. If the student she points out is Student X, the round ends and another begins with different students in the key roles. If the Locator cannot correctly identify Student X after three guesses, her turn ends; then the Navigator reveals the identity of Student X and a new round begins.

World Geography Datelines

For a world geography activity that also familiarizes students with current events, post a large world map at a center. Also place a supply of old newspapers, an atlas, glue, construction paper, pushpins, and a pair of scissors at the center. During free time, a student clips a dateline from a newspaper; then he glues it to a small strip of construction paper. Finally he uses an atlas to find the location of the dateline on the world map. When he locates the city/country, he pins the dateline to its location on the map. Challenge your class to search for datelines that aren't yet pinned on the map.

Mental Maps

Do your students know that they always carry a set of maps in their heads wherever they go? These mental maps help them to get around the school grounds as well as find their sock drawers each morning. Have students brainstorm a list of the mental maps that help them daily. For example, they each have mental maps that help them find the bathroom from the classroom and navigate their own bedrooms in the dark. Instruct each student to select a different mental map to illustrate on a cloud-shaped cutout. Arrange these illustrations on a bulletin board around a large head cutout as shown.

Aarg! I know Africa goes here somewhere!

Mapmaker, Mapmaker, Make Me A Map

Test the accuracy of your students' global mental maps with this activity. Give each student a large sheet of construction paper. Instruct the student to make a map of the world by tearing the paper into shapes to form the seven continents. Have the student glue his continents in their correct positions on another sheet of paper; then have him label the continents and oceans on the map. After assessing your students' knowledge of the position and location of the continents and oceans, save the maps. Then repeat this exercise later in the year to see if your students' mental maps have improved.

Geography Hide-'N'-Seek

Employ a little mystery to reinforce the use of latitude and longitude. Duplicate the map on page 34 for each student. Using a hole puncher, punch circles from heavy paper; then give about 20 to each student. Have one student, the *Hider,* come to the front of the class with his map and place a marker on a latitude/longitude intersection on his map, hiding the location from the class's view. Instruct the other students—the *Seekers*—to take turns guessing the location by calling out latitude/longitude coordinates. Help students keep track of coordinates that have been guessed by writing them on the board and having students mark them on their maps. Instruct the Hider to reveal any parts of the guess that are correct. For example, if the hidden location is 45°N/60°E and a Seeker guesses, "15°S/30°E," the Hider can reply, "One of the directions you named [E] is correct." The next Seeker takes note of that hint and guesses, "45°N/45°E." Since both directions and the latitude degree are correct, the Hider replies, "Both of the directions and the latitude are correct." Play continues until the hidden location is identified. The first Seeker to identify the location becomes the Hider for the next round.

Cap'n... wrong game, ...wrong game!

I sunk your battleship!

What If I Lived There?

Take students on a spin around the world to test their critical-thinking skills. Set your class globe on a table and gently spin it. In turn, have each student stop the spinning globe with one finger. If the student's finger doesn't land on water or his own home region, have him make the following predictions about the spot on the globe he has pinpointed:

- What kinds of land, climate, and seasons does this region have?
- What kinds of people inhabit this region of the world?
- What kinds of clothes do the people wear? What kinds of food do they eat?
- What kinds of animals inhabit this region?
- How do people use the land and water in this region?
- How have people adapted to or changed the environment so that they could live comfortably in this region?

Invite students to share and discuss their predictions. Then have each student research his location and compare his findings with his predictions. Finally ask students to draw some conclusions about regions and people based on their research and discussions.

Landforms	Bodies Of Water
coast	bay
peninsula	strait
canyon	gulf
plateau	harbor
mesa	ocean
continent	lake
basin	river
mountain range	stream
hill	falls
cliff	delta
island	sea
valley	
volcano	
plain	
desert	
isthmus	
swamp	
volcano	

Landform Models

Put your students' creative talents to work by having them construct landform models. Copy the chart of landforms and bodies of water shown at the left on the chalkboard. Challenge each student to create a model that shows at least five landforms and three bodies of water. Allow the student to choose his own materials for this project: clay, salt dough, recycled materials, paper and cardboard, papier maché, or a combination of these materials. Instruct the student to label each landform on his map. If desired have the student attach index-card labels telling how each landform was formed and where examples of each can be found in the world. Show off the completed projects in the school foyer or media center under a banner reading "Shaping Up With Landforms."

Pam Crane

Dream Vacation

Where on Earth would your students like to go on a dream vacation? Begin by brainstorming the types of questions that a typical tourist would want answered, such as, "What's the weather like? Which historical sites are located there? What language is spoken?" Duplicate a copy of the brochure form on page 37 for each student. Have each student research a place she's never visited and write one or two facts about the place on each section of the brochure; then have her fold the brochure on the dotted lines and add the following information to the outside flaps:

Outside front flap (brochure cover): Include the name of the location and an illustration of it.

Outside back flap: Copy and complete the phrase "For more information on _____ [location name], contact the following travel agent: _____ [student name]." Add a short bibliography of books and other resources available in the school's media center.

Display the brochures in a small, open suitcase that's been packed with a few travel clothes, travel magazines, old airline tickets, etc.

Sunny SICILY

Land Regions

A geographic region is defined by its physical and human characteristics. Five distinctive land regions are the *desert, polar, plains, mountain,* and *rainforest* regions. By adapting to the climate, humans can live in all five regions. Divide your class into five teams and assign each team one of the regions. Give each team a three-foot-long sheet of bulletin-board paper. Instruct each team to cut the paper into a giant shape that symbolizes its region. Possible shapes include: a giant saguaro cactus for *desert,* an igloo for *polar,* a tornado for *plains,* a craggy mountain for *mountain,* and a tall, canopied tree for *rainforest.* Instruct each group to record facts about its region on the top half of its cutout. In the center of the cutout, have the group list places around the world that are examples of that region. At the bottom of the cutout, have the group list ways that humans adapt to or change the environment in order to live in that region. Invite each group to share its completed project while showing the locations of the sample regions on a world map.

source → stream → silt → tributaries → river → riverbed → riverbanks → river basin → current → sandbars → canyon → course → flood → delta → mouth

To Be, Or Not To Be...A River

Which landform has played a key role in transportation, trade, travel, agriculture, and energy? The *river,* of course. And for these reasons people have often settled along rivers. Small or great, rivers change the land as they wind their way along. Introduce your students to rivers by role-playing the life of a river. Duplicate "The River Runs" on page 36 for each student. This skit is designed for 20 to 30 students. Establish the teacher or a student as the narrator. Assign the remaining parts based on your class size and the number of students suggested. To prompt students as they act, write the sequence shown above on the board.

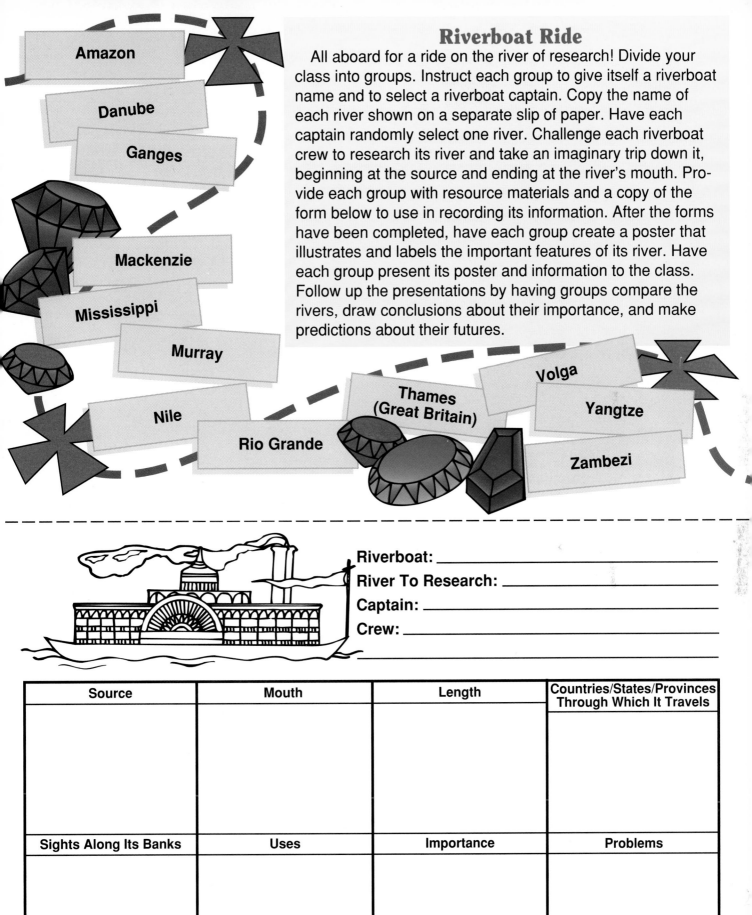

Riverboat Ride

All aboard for a ride on the river of research! Divide your class into groups. Instruct each group to give itself a riverboat name and to select a riverboat captain. Copy the name of each river shown on a separate slip of paper. Have each captain randomly select one river. Challenge each riverboat crew to research its river and take an imaginary trip down it, beginning at the source and ending at the river's mouth. Provide each group with resource materials and a copy of the form below to use in recording its information. After the forms have been completed, have each group create a poster that illustrates and labels the important features of its river. Have each group present its poster and information to the class. Follow up the presentations by having groups compare the rivers, draw conclusions about their importance, and make predictions about their futures.

Amazon

Danube

Ganges

Mackenzie

Mississippi

Murray

Nile

Rio Grande

Thames (Great Britain)

Volga

Yangtze

Zambezi

Riverboat: _____

River To Research: _____

Captain: _____

Crew: _____

Source	Mouth	Length	Countries/States/Provinces Through Which It Travels
Sights Along Its Banks	**Uses**	**Importance**	**Problems**

How Far Is It?

Students can't go the distance in using maps until they know how to use a map scale. Duplicate "How Far Is It?" on page 35 for each student to complete as practice on this important skill. After students complete the reproducible, collect maps that use different scales. Divide the class into cooperative groups and give each group one map. Instruct each group to label a sheet of paper with the title of the map and then write five word problems using the map and its scale. Have the group record its solutions on a separate sheet of paper labeled with the title of the map. Collect the maps, problems, and solutions. Give each group a different map and set of matching word problems to solve. Rotate the maps and problems until each group has seen every map. Check the answers as a class.

Geography Bee

Test your students' geographic know-how by conducting a Geography Bee. Begin by compiling a list of questions and answers, using resource books such as *Everything Is Somewhere: The Geography Quiz Book* by Jack McClintock and David Helgren, Ph.D. (William Morrow & Co., Inc.). Or have students use almanacs and other books to devise their own questions. For a class of 25 students, collect about 150 questions. Add nine questions for every extra student after that. Type the questions and answers on paper. Set two tables with two chairs each at the front of the class.

Conduct the bee in three rounds.

Round 1: Invite the first four students to come to the tables with papers and pencils. Ask the first question, marking it off your list as you do. Allow two minutes for the contestants to write their answers. Call time and ask each contestant to give his answer; then give the correct answer. Award one point to each contestant who gave the correct response. After asking three questions, have four different students come to the tables. Continue play until all students have answered three questions. Any child who gave at least two correct answers during Round 1 moves on to Round 2.
Round 2: Ask three questions of each contestant group as before. Students with at least two correct answers move on to Round 3.
Round 3: Play continues as before. If you need to eliminate contestants at a faster rate, require them to answer all three questions correctly.

Call an end to the bee when there are only three contestants left. Reward all students for their participation, with special honors to the three finalists.

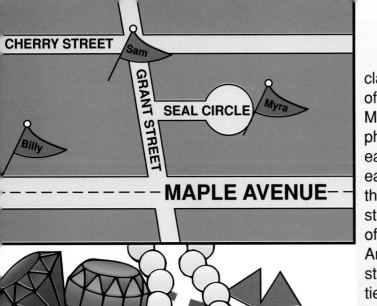

There's No Place Like Home...

...When it comes to learning map skills! Create a classroom learning center by posting a street map of your community on a bulletin board or wall. Make sure the map has a map scale. Place a local phone book next to the map. Write the name of each student on a small, paper triangle; then tape each triangle to the top of a long straight pin. Place the pins on the map to plot the location of each student's home. Use another pin to plot the location of your school. Duplicate a class set of "Tooling Around The Town" on page 39. Instruct each student to complete the required number of activities, using this map and the local phone book.

Debate The Issues

Part of the study of geography involves looking at the relationship between people and their environments. Since the beginning of time, people have adapted to and made changes in their environments. Sometimes individual needs or desires conflict with the workings of the environment.

Listed below are issues that involve people and their environments. Divide your class into five groups. Duplicate the list below; then cut apart the individual issues and give one to each group. Have each group list the pros and cons for both sides of its issue; then have students determine if there is a compromise that the two sides could settle on. Rotate issues between groups so that each group looks at at least three of the issues. Then come together as a class and discuss the issues.

Issue #1:
A group wants to take a natural public area and turn it into a sports field for the townspeople to use. Local nature lovers and hikers disagree.

Issue #2:
A utility company wants to build a dam across a river and build a power plant on the site. The plant will lower the cost of electricity for the city. Farmers downstream are strongly opposed to the plan.

Issue #3:
A local airport wants to expand its runway so that larger planes can land. Local businesses want the business that the extra plane traffic would bring to the area. Area residents—who are already complaining about the noise from the current planes—are strongly opposed to the expansion.

Issue #4:
A city neighborhood group wants to knock down an old building and put in trees and benches for a park area. Local businesspeople want a parking lot on the site. The Historical Committee wants to save and restore the old building.

Issue #5:
A group in town wants to develop a natural beach area into a public beach with bathhouses and a refreshment stand. A local Wildlife Protection group is strongly opposed because this natural beach area is the nesting site of a native bird.

Map

Use with "Geography Hide-'N'-Seek" on page 28. Have each student color the equator red and the prime meridian green.

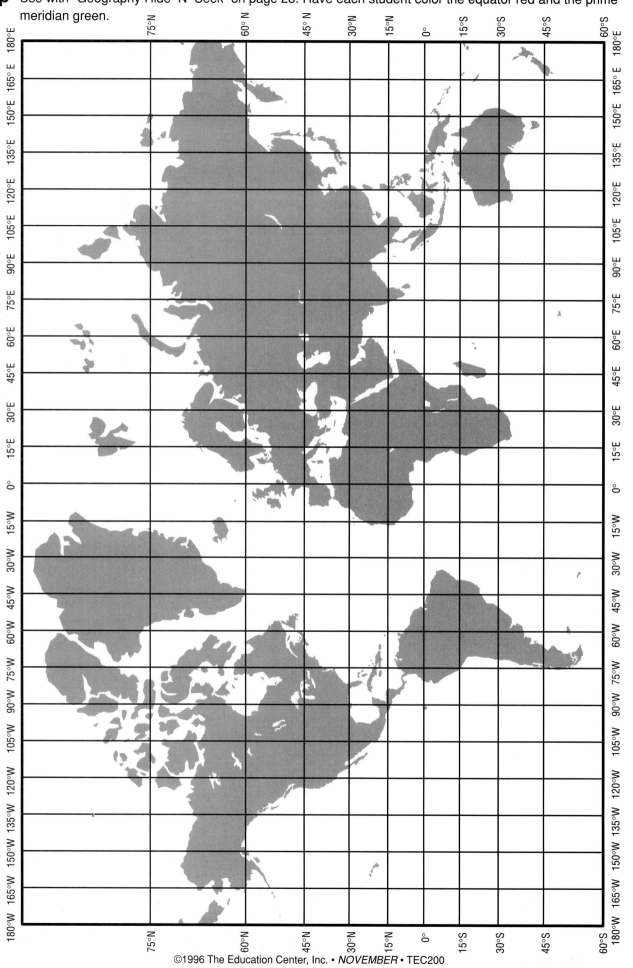

How Far Is It?

Calculating the distance between places on a map is easy if you know how to use the scale. The steps below explain how.

1. Mark a piece of paper to show the distance between the two points (Step 1).
2. Place the paper along the map's scale. Line up the left mark with the zero on the scale (Step 2).
3. If the map scale is shorter than the distance, mark on the paper the endpoint of the scale and the distance it represents. Then line up that endpoint with the zero on the scale (Step 3). Estimate the additional distance according to the scale. Add the two distances to find the total.

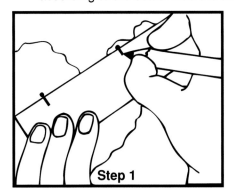
Step 1

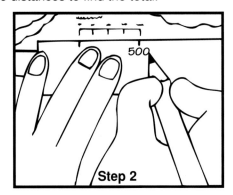
Step 2

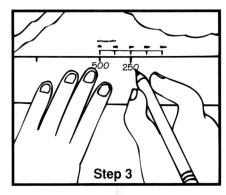
Step 3

Directions: Use a ruler to draw straight lines connecting the points on the map in ABC order. Use the map scale to find the distance between each two cities (the distance between city A and city B, between city B and city C, between city C and city D, etc.). You may use either miles or kilometers. Write the distance between two points on the line that connects them. The first one is done for you.

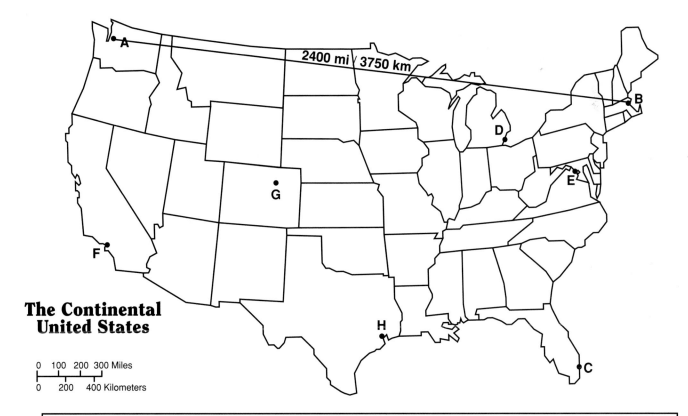

The Continental United States

2400 mi 3750 km

0 100 200 300 Miles

0 200 400 Kilometers

Bonus Box: Each of the points on this map stands for an important city. Compare the map to an atlas. Identify each city by its location on the map. Write your guesses on the back of this page.

Note To The Teacher: Use this page with "How Far Is It?" on page 32. Each student will need a ruler and an atlas or a U.S. map to complete the activity.

The River Runs

Follow your teacher's directions to conduct this river skit.

Narrator: *(Reading slowly and pausing to allow the students time to act out the boldfaced words)*

The **source,** or beginning, of many rivers is in the mountains where collected rain, melting snow, or springwaters form a **stream.** This stream flows downhill—carrying soil, or **silt,** and rock along with it while it carves out a path. Other rivers and streams, called **tributaries** or branches, join it and make it larger. It is now called a **river.**

The bottom of the river is called the **bed**. The sides are called the **banks.** The land area from which all of this water comes is called the **river basin.**

At times—when the land is flat—the river **current** slows down and drops some of the sand and rocks it has been carrying. These deposits can form **sandbars,** or small islands, in the river. Over long periods of time, swift river currents can erode the soil and rock of the riverbed. This erosion forms a **canyon.**

The river's path, or **course,** can sometimes shift and change directions, wandering across the land. Where riverbanks are low or when there is a lot of rain, the river will **flood** the land that surrounds it.

As a river approaches the sea, it drops its silt and forms a wide area of fertile, built-up land called a **delta.** This is the river's **mouth,** where it reaches its final destination, the sea.

Key Word	Actions By Student(s)
Source	One student stands on a table or counter as a mountain.
Stream	A new student climbs up next to the source and slowly climbs down. This student will lead the river all the way to the mouth. She waves a blue streamer in each hand.
Silt	Two students join the stream, tumbling behind it.
Tributaries	Two students come from different directions and join up behind the original stream. They each hold streamers in their hands.
River	The stream and tributary students now make up the river and continue moving in a line together.
Riverbed	Two new students lie on the floor as the stream passes by.
Riverbanks	Two new students on each side of the riverbed (four students in all) kneel on the floor, arms out to their sides.
River Basin	Four new students fan out in a semicircle from the sides of the river to form the riverbed.
Current	The river students continue to walk slowly.
Sandbars	One of the silt students deposits himself on the floor and no longer follows the river.
Canyon	Two new students on each side of the river (four new students in all) stand on chairs with arms outstretched.
Course	The river students slowly zigzag along between the canyon walls.
Flood	Two of the river students walk off to the sides waving arms in all directions, then rejoin the main river student(s).
Delta	Three new students form a triangle, arms outstretched. The remaining silt student sits down and no longer follows the river.
Mouth	Two students stand with hands on hips to indicate the sea. The river students walk past the delta and sea students.

©1996 The Education Center, Inc. • *NOVEMBER* • TEC200

Note To The Teacher: Use this page with "To Be, Or Not To Be…A River" on page 30. You will need one sturdy table or counter; four chairs; and a pair of three-foot-long, light blue crepe-paper streamers for each *river* student (optional).

Dream Vacation Brochure

Use with "Dream Vacation" on page 29. Have the student cut out the brochure before folding it.

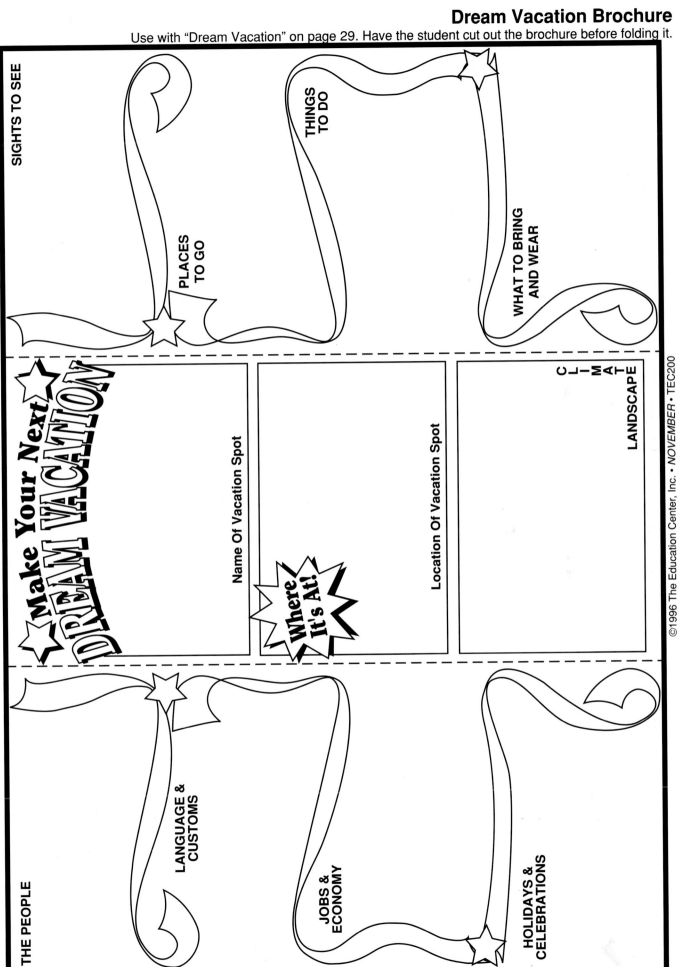

SIGHTS TO SEE

PLACES TO GO

THINGS TO DO

WHAT TO BRING AND WEAR

Make Your Next DREAM VACATION

Name Of Vacation Spot

Where It's At!

Location Of Vacation Spot

CLIMATE

LANDSCAPE

THE PEOPLE

LANGUAGE & CUSTOMS

JOBS & ECONOMY

HOLIDAYS & CELEBRATIONS

Piecing It Together

Our great nation is huge and is made up of several different regions. Pieced together these regions make up one whole country! Color the key to assign a different color to each region. Then use a resource book or your textbook to help you color each state according to the region in which it's located.

When you've finished coloring the map, number a sheet of paper 1–50. Write the name of each state and its capital on the paper, using the map as your guide.

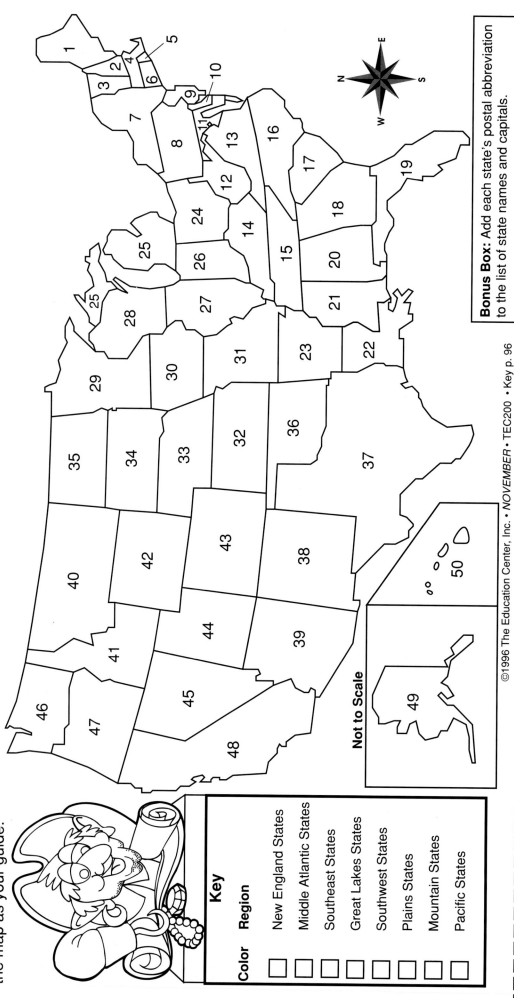

Not to Scale

Key

Color	Region
☐	New England States
☐	Middle Atlantic States
☐	Southeast States
☐	Great Lakes States
☐	Southwest States
☐	Plains States
☐	Mountain States
☐	Pacific States

Bonus Box: Add each state's postal abbreviation to the list of state names and capitals.

Note To The Teacher: Students will need an atlas or a U.S. map and colored pencils or crayons.

Tooling Around The Town

Complete ____ of the following activities by ____. Write your answers on your own paper and staple them to this contract.

1. Look at the locations of student homes on the map. Which two students do you estimate live farthest apart?

2. Using the map key, make a list of the different kinds of roads shown on the map (interstate highway, two-lane, one-way, paved, etc.). What kind of road do you live on?

3. Use the map's scale to determine how many miles it is from your school to your home if you travel in a straight line.

4. Write directions that would help someone from school get to your house. Be sure to include street names and directions about where to turn left or right. Include one or two landmarks too.

5. Locate two different shopping malls or centers in your community. Measure the distance between your home and each of the malls. Which mall is closer to your home? At which mall would your family be more likely to shop? Why?

6. Select the locations of five classmates who live in different neighborhoods. Write sentences describing where each student lives in relation to the school and one of the other five classmates. For example, "Sid lives northeast of the school and south of Madeline."

7. Select the location of a classmate who lives far from you. Study the streets that run between your two homes. Write directions telling that student how to get to your house from his or her house.

8. Locate the fire station closest to your home. Estimate the number of miles (by road) that fire trucks would have to travel to get to your house. Would the trucks have to travel through city streets, on highways, or on country roads to get to your house? How would these streets help—or would they keep the truck from getting quickly to your home?

9. Using the phone book, list the names and addresses of the following businesses: a doctor's office, a movie theater, a restaurant, a plumbing company, and a library. Use the map's index of streets to locate each business. Place a pin on each business's location on the map. Have the teacher or a classmate check your work. Remove the five pins when you have finished.

10. Estimate the number of miles you would travel if you walked the entire perimeter (outside edges) of your town.

©1996 The Education Center, Inc. • NOVEMBER • TEC200

39

Note To The Teacher: Use this page with "There's No Place Like Home…" on page 33. Read over the activities before assigning this page so that you can change or eliminate any that do not match your town map. Before duplicating, fill in the blanks with the number of required activities and the due date.

Setting The Stage For American Education Week!

Activities For A Unique Celebration Of Education

American Education Week, observed the week before Thanksgiving, focuses attention on public education. Explore the topic of schools during this special week—and honor the people who make yours tick—with the following thematic activities.

by Peggy W. Hambright

Classy Books

Jump-start your celebration of American Education Week by reading aloud a humorous, informational, or biographical book that features the theme of education. Ask your media specialist to recommend a book, or choose one from the list below.

Fiction:
- *Heads Or Tails: Stories From The Sixth Grade* by Jack Gantos (Farrar, Straus & Giroux, Inc.; 1994)
- *Wayside School Is Falling Down* by Louis Sachar (Avon Books, 1990)
- *Wayside School Gets A Little Stranger* by Louis Sachar (Morrow Junior Books, 1995)
- *My Teacher Fried My Brains* by Bruce Coville (Minstrel Books, 1991)
- *Sixth Grade Can Really Kill You* by Barthe DeClements (Puffin Books, 1995)
- *The Best School Year Ever* by Barbara Robinson (HarperCollins Children's Books, 1994)

Informational:
- *A One-Room School* by Bobbie Kalman (Crabtree Publishing Company, 1994)
- *Early Schools* by Bobbie Kalman (Crabtree Publishing Company, 1982)

Biographies:
- *What Do You Mean? A Story About Noah Webster* by Jeri Ferris (Carolrhoda Books, 1988)
- *Mary McLeod Bethune* by Malu Halasa (Chelsea House, 1993)

Meet Our Cast

In honor of American Education Week, supplement the reading material in your school office's reception area with a who's who of staff members! Have your students photograph and interview every staff member—teachers, assistants, cafeteria workers, custodial staff, bus drivers, office personnel—in your school. Have the students ask staff members the questions shown, or have interviewees fill out a questionnaire to return. Next have the students organize the photos and responses into a scrapbook, decorate its cover, and present it to the principal. Visitors waiting to speak with the principal will have a ready reference on the folks who really make your school tick!

Who's Who

Name: Mrs. Hinkle
Position: 5th-grade teacher
Why do you like working with children? They are so honest!
What is the most challenging part of your job? Making every day fun, interesting, and loaded with learning.
What is the most rewarding part of your job? Knowing I might have a small part in the molding of a youngster's destiny.
What's the funniest thing that's happened at your job? One day I wore two different shoes to school!

Tell Me 'Bout The Good Ol' Days

Send your students on an intriguing educational journey into what school was like for their older relatives and friends! Have your students invite members of an older generation to visit your classroom. Ask students to tell these folks that they'll be requested to reminisce about what school was like for them. Then use the reproducible on page 52 to prepare for this special event.

If some students' interviewees are not physically able to visit the classroom, encourage each of those students to tape-record or videotape their interview session and then bring it to class to share. Give each child who will be conducting an off-site interview a copy of page 52 to use as a guide.

Recipe For: A Successful School
Written by: Andy

1 dedicated teacher
1 classroom of motivated,
    eager-to-learn kids
Plenty of resources
Parents who care

Mix well. Bake until June!

Student-Written Recipes

Stir up a little critical thinking with a recipe-writing activity! Brainstorm with students ideas that would guarantee a school's success. List the students' ideas on the chalkboard. Give each student a copy of the bottom half of page 50. Direct him to choose "ingredients" from the board that he thinks would make a successful school. Have him write the name of his recipe on the card, list its ingredients, and give the needed directions. Post the recipes on a bulletin board titled "Recipes For A Successful School."

Personalize this project by having each student write how *he* can have a successful school year. Provide the student with a 4" x 6" index card or another copy of the recipe-card reproducible. Ask him to write his own "Recipe For A Successful School Year."

Day-By-Day Accolades

Involve your students in a nifty day-by-day plan to let school staff members—and others—know they're appreciated! Assist students in listing the groups of people who make your school run smoothly: cafeteria workers, office personnel, custodial staff, bus drivers, specialists, teacher assistants, volunteers, etc. Divide your class into teams. Assign each team one or more groups of school helpers. Then follow the game plan below and on page 43 for a week of affirmations and accolades!

PARENT VOLUNTEERS

• MONDAY: Flag-Waving Banners

Have students make flag-waving banners to honor school workers! Have each group make a computer or hand-drawn banner, spelling the honored group's name in large block letters and then coloring it. Direct each team to then make a flag for each person in its group using the following directions:

1. Cut a flag shape from colored construction paper.
2. Write the name of an honoree prominently on the flag.
3. Make cut-out symbols that represent the honoree; then glue them to the flag.
4. Staple a flagpole made from rolled paper to the flag.

Staple each honoree's flag to the banner. Then have representatives from your class present the banners to the staff members.

• TUESDAY: Razzle-Dazzle Posters

Advertise the great job school workers do to make your school terrific! Have each team make a poster to honor its group of workers. Send out teams of students to interview each honoree and find out what his/her job entails. Then have teams illustrate their information on a decorative poster. (Save this information to use again for making "Headliner Cards" on page 43.) Challenge the students to add pizzazz to their posters by using clever phrases or riddles (see the illustration). Mount the posters in the cafeteria, library, or school reception area.

Who ya gonna call when the hamster gets lost?

Our Fearless Custodian, MR. BOST!

• WEDNESDAY: Ego-Boosting Wreaths

Have each team make a poster-board wreath for each honoree in its group. (Or have teams wrap inexpensive Styrofoam® wreaths with crepe paper.) Instruct students to make colorful, cut-out shapes of items each honoree uses to do his/her job. For example, a wreath for the school secretary could show a desk, a telephone, a computer, file folders, a stapler, etc. Have the students glue the shapes onto the wreath. Ask students to also glue a name banner and a loop of ribbon for hanging to each wreath.

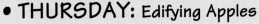

Mrs. Cole is appreciated because she helped me with my math.

Rhonda T.

• THURSDAY: Edifying Apples

Allow your students to express appreciation to individual school workers with this "apple-tizing" project! List the names of specific individuals your class wants to honor on the chalkboard. (Keep the list to four to six names.) Brainstorm with students the ways that these school workers help them. Give each student a copy of the apple pattern on the top half of page 50. Direct the student to select one person from the list, write his/her name on the apple, and then describe a time when this person really helped him. Staple all cutouts written about the same individual behind an apple-shaped cover (made by tracing the apple pattern onto red paper) labeled with the honoree's name. Select class representatives to deliver the apple booklets to the honorees.

• FRIDAY: Headliner Cards

Transform interesting trivia about school workers' jobs into headline news! Using the same teams described in "Day-By-Day Accolades" on page 42, have each team choose one person from its group of workers to honor. Challenge the team to capture the gist of that person's job description in a one-of-a-kind greeting card. Have each team follow these directions for making its card:

1. Fold an 8 1/2" x 11" sheet of gray construction paper in half.
2. Print a headline across the top of the card.
3. Draw a line that creates two vertical columns in the remaining space.
4. Write a *brief* article that describes the person's job, leaving space for an illustration. (Have students refer to the information they gathered during interviews for "Razzle-Dazzle Posters" on page 42.)
5. Write a personal message on the inside of the card.

Appoint a "postman" to deliver the cards and report on how they were received!

School Secretary Answers Over 50 Calls Each Day!

Mrs. Jones has worked at our school for 18 years. She says she has loved every day! She answers the phone and greets visitor

She also types letters and reports for the principal and teachers.

This is the 54th call today!

43

Decorated Doors

Invite your school to participate in an educational door-decorating contest for American Education Week! Ask every teacher in grades three and up to choose a name from the list of great American educators on page 51. Direct the teacher to have her class research the educator's life and choose highlights of his/her career to feature on her classroom door. Ask the teacher to cover her door with background paper. Direct her to have her students illustrate high points from the educator's life and attach them to the door. After each classroom's door has been completed, suggest that teachers cruise the halls with their classes so that students can view all of the doors. Ask the principal, PTA president, and school secretary to act as judges for the contest. Treat the winning class to a gift certificate (donated by a local educational store) to purchase something that the entire class can enjoy.

NOAH WEBSTER

Publisher   Teacher
Author   Lawyer

American Magazine

American Spelling

The Dictionary

A Quilt Of Educators

Propose that your class take on a quilt-making project in honor of American Education Week. Have each student choose a different name from the list of great American educators on page 51 to research. Give each student an 11-inch white-paper doily. Ask that the student draw a portrait of his person or a picture illustrating his/her achievements to glue on the doily. Have each child glue his doily to a 14-inch square of colored construction paper. Then have the student add a one-sentence summary of his educator's major accomplishments. Direct each student to punch a hole in each corner of his paper. Have him tie his summary to those of his classmates with yarn to make a class quilt. Hang the quilt proudly on a classroom wall or in a hallway near the front door of the school.

Mary McLeod Bethune improved educational opportunities for blacks.

Letters Of Remembrance

Honor favorite teachers during American Education Week with this letter-writing activity. Ask each student to write a letter to the teacher he feels had the greatest influence on him. Suggest that the letter mention specific ways that this particular teacher made learning more fun or interesting. To help a student who's new to your class get in touch with a favorite teacher from his previous school, consult his permanent-records folder for an address. Or have the student write a thank-you letter to the person who helped make the transition to his new school easier. For a different twist, ask each student to write a letter to a future teacher—one he hopes to have *next* year. See that all letters are mailed or delivered.

Dear Mrs. Mitchell,
  You were the teacher who helped me to really enjoy school. You didn't just tell us about something—you let us do it! I still remember making ice cream in a can!
  Thanks for everything.

Love,
Scott

Grade-Level Memoirs

Provide a forum for remembering the terrific times of previous school years with a fun book-making project! Assign each student the task of writing about his fondest school memories by grade level. For example, if a student is presently in fifth grade, ask him to write his memories of fourth grade on one piece of unlined paper, memories of third grade on another sheet, and so on until he has retraced his way to kindergarten. Distribute colored pencils so that the student can add illustrations to each page. Then have the student staple his memoirs inside a decorated cover. See the next idea for a terrific way to share these student-made books!

Lunch And More

Invite parents to do more than eat and run when they have lunch at school during American Education Week. Ask parents to join your class for a time either before or after the lunch period. During this special session, have students read the keepsake books they made in "Grade-Level Memoirs" above. Parents will love seeing their children's published memoirs and hearing them read. And since this is a sharing session, how about suggesting that parents share *their* favorite classroom memories with the class too?

A School Day From Yesteryear

Step back into time and let your students experience what a one-room school was like generations ago! Adapt some of your "reading, 'riting, and 'rithmetic" plans so that they include the reproducible on page 49 as well as the activities that follow:

- **Make a hornbook:** Give each student a desktop-size piece of cardboard and have him draw on it the shape of a paddle. Assist the student with cutting out the shape. Have the student glue a sheet of white paper to one side of the cardboard paddle and trim off the excess. Let the student use his hornbook for completing one or more assignments during the day.
- **Write on a slate:** Give each child a small, desk-size chalkboard, a piece of chalk, and a paper towel. Ask the student to write answers to review problems or questions posed by you on his slate. After holding up his chalkboard to show a response, have each child wipe it clean with his paper towel and get ready for another round.
- **Recite:** Assign students a short poem to memorize and recite for the class. Or select a brief, seasonal choral reading for students to say as a group.
- **Participate in a spelling bee:** Let your students practice the week's spelling words with a spelling bee.

To give your students a different perspective, share some of the standards that teachers were expected to maintain during the 1870s, as shown on the right. Then let your class share its opinions of these standards!

1872
Standards For Teachers

1. Female teachers who marry will lose their jobs.
2. Male teachers may date one evening a week——or two evenings if they are regular church attenders.
3. After working for five years, a teacher who maintains all standards and works faithfully will receive a pay raise of twenty-five cents per week.

Teacher-To-Teacher

American Education Week is the perfect time to do something special for your teaching colleagues. Try one of these ways to say, "I think you're great!":

- Fill an inexpensive mug with change for the soda machine, instant cocoa or tea packets, mints, sugarless candies, and a new pen.
- Surprise a teaching colleague with a certificate good for one 30-minute period of recess duty.
- During one of your students' special classes, pop into a colleague's room with a terrific picture book (appropriate for older students) or a collection of humorous poetry. Offer to read to her class for 10 minutes while she takes a break.
- Treat yourself, as well as a colleague, by taking a 20-minute walk together around the school grounds after school. Offer to supply iced-down bottled water for an after-walk refreshment.
- Offer to be responsible for decorating one of your colleague's bulletin boards for the next month.
- For fun, have each cooperative group in your class draw a life-sized diagram of "The Perfect Teacher," complete with labels and descriptions. Post the diagrams in your faculty room.

A Sticky Reminder

Share positive messages about education by making one-of-a-kind window stickers! Give each child a nine-inch square of tagboard. Have the student draw and cut out a large, school-related shape (apple, pencil, notebook, etc.) from the tagboard. Direct the student to cut four 4-inch strips of construction paper, fold them accordion style, and then glue them to his cutout as shown. Have the student write a brief, catchy message about education on his cutout; then have him use markers to add finishing touches. Send a small square of Plasti-Tak® home with each student. Instruct the student to attach a small piece to the end of each folded strip, then mount his sticker on a side rear window of his family's car.

If you've thanked a teacher today, **HONK!**

THANK$ A MILLION!

Dear Taxpayer,
I have really enjoyed learning how to use the computer. I use it to write stories, poems, and reports. I like to print my copies in color. I also practice my math skills on the computer.
My whole class got new desks this year, too!
Sincerely,
Scott

ONE DOLLAR

Thanks A Million!

Give thanks where it's due by having students praise the taxpayers whose dollars support our country's schools. Explain to students some of the ways that tax dollars are used each year to help schools (provide new computers, playground equipment, art supplies, textbooks, library resources, etc.; pay teachers' salaries; build new school buildings, etc.). Photograph each student using an item provided by tax dollars. Have each student trim his photo and glue it to the center of a 5" x 11" sheet of light green construction paper. Ask the student to use the remaining space to write a letter to a taxpayer expressing his appreciation for the opportunity to attend school and use its resources. Direct the student to add details to make his photo/letter resemble a dollar bill. Then have him staple it to a slightly larger sheet of black paper. Display the students' letters on a bulletin board titled "Thanks A Million!"

LOOK
Whooo Will Visit...

The mayor will visit today
from 10:30–11:00 A.M.

Honored Guests

Invite local people who are both interesting and successful to speak to your class during American Education Week. For example, ask a well-known high-school student, a respected community leader, someone recognized for her service to others, or a local politician to give a motivational talk. Plan for this person to talk about the opportunities that were available to her because of her education, and how these opportunities helped advance her career. Encourage your students to ask questions.

After the visit, ask students to write paragraphs summarizing what they learned and predicting how they might apply this information to their own lives. Post these summaries on a bulletin board titled "Looking To The Future."

The Look Of Success

What does a successful student look like? Pose this question to your class, and you're likely to hear comments that focus on physical appearance or clothing. Help students understand that it's a successful student's actions—not his clothes—that result in the perception he desires others to have of him. Would a successful student think about reading a comic book during class or concentrate on finding a solution to a math problem? Would a successful student watch a science demonstration carefully or would he try to get his neighbor's attention? After discussing the attributes of a successful student with your class, give each child a copy of the reproducible activity "The Look Of Success" on page 53 to complete. Or have each group draw a life-size outline of a student's body on a piece of butcher paper and add labels as shown on the reproducible.

In The Year 2125

Project your students into the future and have them imagine what school will be like in the 22nd century! Have students focus on the following:

- What will a school of the future look like in terms of architecture and design?
- How will students be transported between home and school?
- How involved will technology be in education and learning?
- How will instruction be given—by humans, robots, or machines?
- Will virtual reality be involved with the learning process? If so, how?
- What subjects will be obsolete—and if so, which subjects will replace them?

After each student has written about what he believes schools will be like in the future, have him make a model or drawing of his futuristic school. Display the students' writings and artwork in the library during American Education Week.

P. S. 2125

A School Day From Yesteryear

What was it like to attend a one-room school during the 1800s? For one thing, children of all ages and abilities worked together in one room, taught by one teacher. The books used were the *Bible* and a *primer*, a book for teaching children to read, spell, and use numbers. Lots of time was spent memorizing and reciting lessons and poems. Children also wrote and delivered speeches. In some schools, *hornbooks* were used. A hornbook looked like a wooden paddle. A piece of paper that contained a written lesson was attached to it. It had a protective film over it that made it last a long time. A popular reading book was the McGuffey Reader. It taught lessons on manners and values as well as reading.

Children spent hours practicing their handwriting. To write, a child scratched on a slate board with a slate pencil. If he could afford one, he wrote in a copybook. A copybook's paper was blank so the child had to draw his own lines on the paper first. Students also used a sharpened goose-feather pen called a *quill*. This type of pen left a lot of wet ink on the page, so children had to cover each page with blotting paper after writing. The blotting paper absorbed the extra ink and prevented smudges.

Compare your school to a one-room school by answering these questions on the back of this page.

1. How do the books you use at school differ from the ones described for a one-room school?

2. Tell how your writing tools and paper are like the ones used long ago. How are they different?

3. What kinds of problems do you think a teacher would have with teaching different-aged children in just one room?

4. The McGuffey Readers taught children more than just how to read. Good manners and values like honesty and courage were also taught through its stories. How do children today learn these things?

5. Why do you think neat handwriting was so important during this time in history?

6. Why do you think speech making was such an important part of learning during this time?

7. Would you have liked to attend school during this time in history? Why or why not?

8. Would you have liked to be a teacher in a one-room school? Why or why not?

Bonus Box: List the letters of the alphabet on another sheet of paper, one letter per line. Beside each letter, write the name of a school-related item that begins with that letter. Use items from modern times or from the past.

Note To The Teacher: Use this reproducible with "A School Day From Yesteryear" on page 46.

Patterns

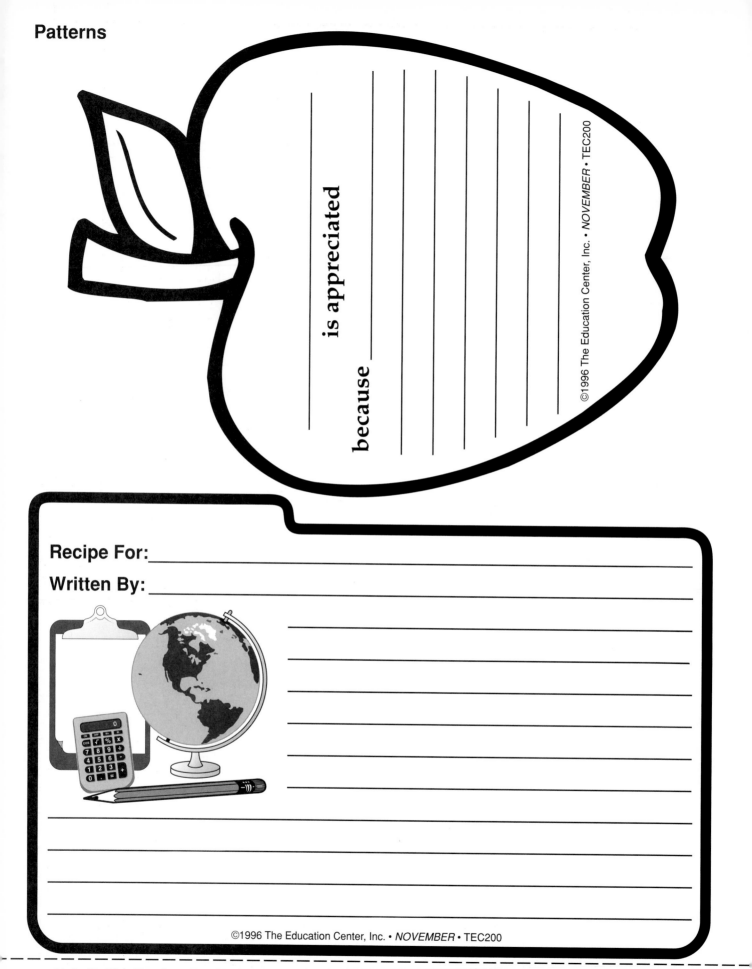

is appreciated

because

©1996 The Education Center, Inc. • *NOVEMBER* • TEC200

Recipe For:_____

Written By:_____

Great American Educators

Name	Birth/Death	Major Contribution
Charles B. Aycock	1859–1912	Established rural high schools and teacher-training schools.
Martha M. Berry	1866–1942	Established schools for poor Southern mountain people.
Mary McLeod Bethune	1875–1955	Improved educational opportunities for blacks.
Nicholas M. Butler	1862–1947	Founded Columbia University's Teachers College.
Mary Ann S. Cary	1823–1893	Taught in and established schools for blacks.
Hollis L. Caswell	1901–1988	Was an authority on curriculum planning.
James Bryant Conant	1893–1978	Recommended changes for teaching high-school math, science, and foreign languages.
Prudence Crandall	1803–1890	Opened a Connecticut school for black girls.
Jabez L. M. Curry	1825–1903	Worked to obtain education for all children—black and white—in the South.
Charles W. Eliot	1834–1926	Recommended standard high-school courses.
Thomas H. Gallaudet	1787–1851	Founded the Hartford School for the Deaf.
Edward M. Gallaudet	1837–1917	Was president of the Columbia Institution for the Deaf and the Dumb and the Blind (now Gallaudet College).
John R. Gregg	1867–1948	Founded a school to teach his shorthand method of writing and other business subjects.
G. Stanley Hall	1844–1924	Explained how child psychology experiments could be helpful to teachers.
S. I. Hayakawa	1906–1992	Was an expert on *semantics*, the meaning of words.
Phoebe A. Hearst	1842–1919	Established the national organization of local parent-teacher associations (PTAs).
John Hope	1868–1936	Encouraged blacks to attend college rather than vocational school.
Horace Mann	1796–1859	Helped establish elementary schools in the United States.
William H. McGuffey	1800–1873	Published illustrated reading books for elementary schools.
Francis W. Parker	1837–1902	Developed elementary science and geography programs.
George I. Sánchez	1906–1972	Led the fight for educational reforms for Spanish-speaking students in the United States.
B. F. Skinner	1904–1990	Did research on how people learn.
Martha C. Thomas	1857–1935	Fought for equal educational opportunities for women.
Edward L. Thorndike	1874–1949	Designed tests to measure learning and aptitudes.
Booker T. Washington	1856–1915	Founded Tuskegee Institute, a vocational school for blacks.
Noah Webster	1758–1843	Compiled an American English dictionary.

Note To The Teacher: Use this list of educators with "Decorated Doors" and "A Quilt Of Educators" on page 44.

Tell Me 'Bout The Good Ol' Days

Today's schools—some with on-line computers and other types of technology—are very different from those your grandparents and great-grandparents attended. Plan a time when a grandparent or older friend can reminisce with you about what school was like for him/her. Use the questions below to help you with your interview. Then share the answers with your class.

Hints For Conducting A Successful Interview

- Find out in advance all you can about the person you plan to interview.
- Arrange a time and place for the interview.
- Ask a simple question first.
- Ask questions that require more than a *yes* or *no* answer.

- Record the interviewee's answers by taking notes or using a tape recorder.
- Thank the person at the end of the interview.
- Write up the interview and give the person you interviewed a copy to enjoy.

Questions To Ask

1. How did you get to school?
2. What time did your school day begin and end? How many months long was your school year? What holidays were observed?
3. How did kids behave in school back then compared to how they behave in today's schools?
4. Tell me how discipline was handled when you were in school.
5. What were your tests like?
6. Describe the report cards and grading scales your teachers used.
7. What kinds of games did you play at recess? How long did you get for recess?
8. What kinds of school supplies did you have?
9. Tell me about your school cafeteria and the types of food you had.
10. What kinds of desks and books did you have?
11. What styles of clothes and hairstyles were popular when you were in school?
12. Tell me about your music and art classes.
13. Where were your school's bathrooms and water fountains located?
14. Was your school air-conditioned? If not, how did you stay cool?
15. Tell me about your favorite teacher.
16. What was your favorite subject?
17. What was the funniest thing that ever happened to you in school?

Bonus Box: Write up the interview in the form of a script. Begin with an introduction that explains the reason for the interview and gives background information on your relative or friend.

Note To The Teacher: Use this reproducible with "Tell Me 'Bout The Good Ol' Days" on page 41.

The Look Of Success

What do successful students look like? What's inside their heads? What do the eyes of successful students see? What do their ears hear? What do their mouths say? What do the hearts of successful students feel? What do their hands do? Where do their feet take them?

Look at the diagram below. Complete each label to describe the various parts of a successful student. Then decorate and color the figure to make it look like you.

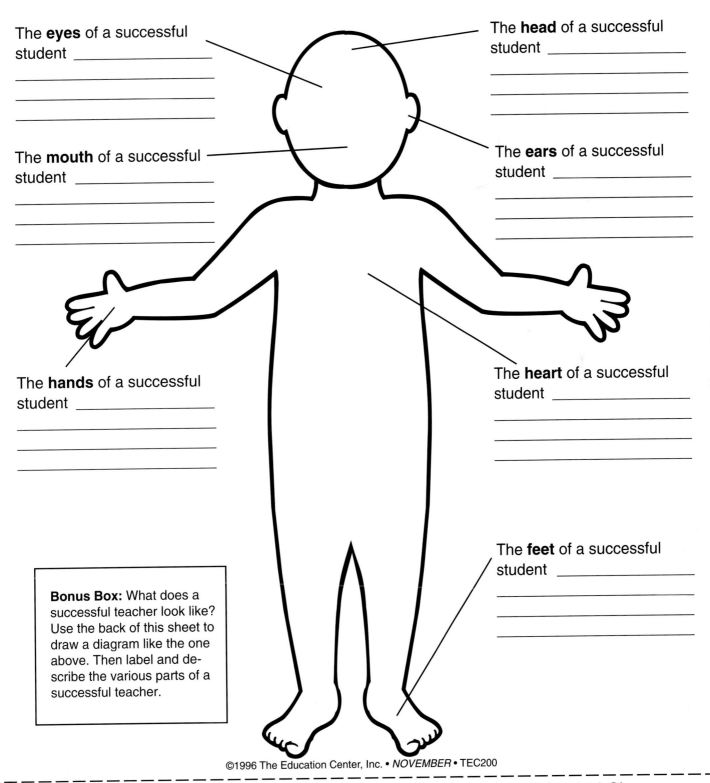

The **eyes** of a successful student _____
_____
_____
_____

The **head** of a successful student _____
_____
_____
_____

The **mouth** of a successful student _____
_____
_____
_____

The **ears** of a successful student _____
_____
_____
_____

The **hands** of a successful student _____
_____
_____
_____

The **heart** of a successful student _____
_____
_____
_____

The **feet** of a successful student _____
_____
_____
_____

Bonus Box: What does a successful teacher look like? Use the back of this sheet to draw a diagram like the one above. Then label and describe the various parts of a successful teacher.

- -

Note To The Teacher: Duplicate one copy of this reproducible for each student to use with "The Look Of Success" on page 48.

Booking A Trip
Reading Activities For Celebrating National Children's Book Week

Make plans now to cruise through National Children's Book Week in November with the help of the following creative activities. Use these terrific ideas—each designed to give students an unsinkable desire to enjoy reading—together as a thematic unit that helps you sail through Book Week. Or pull individual ideas anytime you want to keep students' interest in reading afloat!

by Simone Lepine and Christine Thuman

Ship's Manifest

Booking A Trip

Around The World!

Step Aside, Samsonite®!

Create this colorful bulletin board that serves as the centerpiece of your reading activities! Center a world map on a large board. Enlarge, color, and cut out the cruise ship pattern on page 63 to add to the board as shown. Punch out paper circles with a hole puncher. Then write each student's initials on a punched-out circle and glue it to the top of a pushpin. Store the pins on the board by pushing them in along the border of the map. Instruct each student to cut out a large suitcase shape from a 9" x 12" sheet of colored paper and to add details such as handles and pockets. Post the suitcases around the map.

Duplicate a supply of the Book Week Travel Tags on page 64 and cut them out. Store them in a basket near the bulletin board. Each time a student completes a Book Week activity, instruct her to fill out one tag with her name, the name of the activity, and her destination (a city and country somewhere in the world). To ensure that she travels the world, instruct her to select a different city and continent for each activity. After pasting her tag onto her suitcase, have her move her pushpin to that city on the map. By the end of the unit, she will have collected a tag for each activity and "booked" a trip around the world!

Around The World

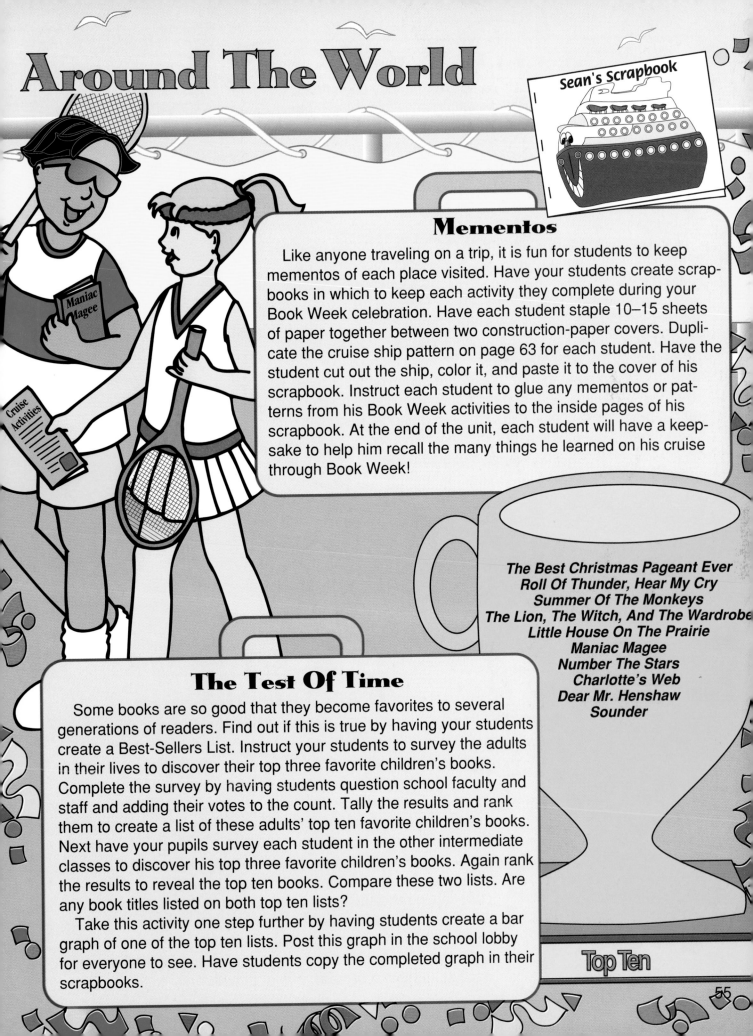

Sean's Scrapbook

Mementos

Like anyone traveling on a trip, it is fun for students to keep mementos of each place visited. Have your students create scrapbooks in which to keep each activity they complete during your Book Week celebration. Have each student staple 10–15 sheets of paper together between two construction-paper covers. Duplicate the cruise ship pattern on page 63 for each student. Have the student cut out the ship, color it, and paste it to the cover of his scrapbook. Instruct each student to glue any mementos or patterns from his Book Week activities to the inside pages of his scrapbook. At the end of the unit, each student will have a keepsake to help him recall the many things he learned on his cruise through Book Week!

The Best Christmas Pageant Ever
Roll Of Thunder, Hear My Cry
Summer Of The Monkeys
The Lion, The Witch, And The Wardrobe
Little House On The Prairie
Maniac Magee
Number The Stars
Charlotte's Web
Dear Mr. Henshaw
Sounder

Top Ten

The Test Of Time

Some books are so good that they become favorites to several generations of readers. Find out if this is true by having your students create a Best-Sellers List. Instruct your students to survey the adults in their lives to discover their top three favorite children's books. Complete the survey by having students question school faculty and staff and adding their votes to the count. Tally the results and rank them to create a list of these adults' top ten favorite children's books. Next have your pupils survey each student in the other intermediate classes to discover his top three favorite children's books. Again rank the results to reveal the top ten books. Compare these two lists. Are any book titles listed on both top ten lists?

Take this activity one step further by having students create a bar graph of one of the top ten lists. Post this graph in the school lobby for everyone to see. Have students copy the completed graph in their scrapbooks.

Ticket To The Future

Do you often hear students complain that they can't find a good book to read? Here's a motivating activity to help them make better reading choices. Duplicate page 65 for each child. Explain that the survey will help each student recognize his interests. Have each student complete the survey; then discuss each of the survey items and ask students to explain their choices. List the books that students noted as their favorites on the board.

Next group students according to the types of books they like to read (mystery, humor, etc.). Have students in each group share the names of books from the group's category that they would recommend to each other. Designate one child from each group to add these titles to the list on the board. Have each student look at this list—and the one generated in "The Test Of Time" activity on page 55—to select three titles he'd like to read. Instruct each student to write these three titles on his "Ticket To The Future" pattern (bottom half of page 65). Have the student cut out his ticket and glue it inside his scrapbook. Each time the student reads one of these books, have him bring his scrapbook to you so that you can stamp the space under the book's title.

Reading Survey		
Mystery	Humor	History Fiction
Adventure	Fantasy	Biography

Book Title Alphabet

Sometimes all it takes to spark interest in new books is to give students a chance to browse the shelves. Add some purpose to your browsing by informing students that they will be creating a Book Title Alphabet. Schedule a visit to the media center. Have each student bring a pencil and a notebook with the letters of the alphabet listed down the side of one sheet of paper. Instruct each student to search the shelves to locate a book title starting with each letter of the alphabet. Remind students that the words *the, a,* and *an* do not count as the beginning of a title, and that the card catalog and the browser are off-limits in this activity! Have each student attach his list of titles, along with authors, to a page in his scrapbook. Then have him draw a star by any book that looks like it might be interesting to read in the future. Reward each student who completes this list with a bookmark.

Snowball Fight

Introduce your students to a variety of authors while releasing some pent-up energy! Gather a supply of intermediate-level books that each have a short biography about the author (one for every two students). For each book, write the author's name on one piece of paper and the book's title on another piece. Wad up each piece of paper and place it in a bag. Have each student pick one of the wadded pieces out of the bag. Then let your class have a 30-second "snowball" fight by throwing the wads of paper at one another in the room. At the end of the fight, make sure each student has one piece of paper. Instruct each student to open her paper to discover if she has an author or a book title; then direct each student to locate the person who holds the matching book title or author.

Once two students think they have found the correct author/title match, instruct them to come to you. If they do not have the correct match, have them go back and look for their rightful partners. Give each correct pair a copy of its book along with instructions to read about the author. Have each student in the pair write down five facts about her author in her scrapbook. Invite each pair to share facts about its author with the class.

Pass the mysteries, please.

I sure would like a second helping of historical fiction!

A Wrinkle In Time

The Boy King

Sounder

Walk Two Moons

Novel Nutrition Facts

Title: *Charlotte's Web*
Author: *E. B. White*

Rating (1–10: 1 = "poor," 10 = "fantastic"): 10
Reasons For Rating: *A real page-turner!*

Amount Per Book	% Value
Fantasy	
Historical Fiction	50
Humor	
Mystery	50
Realistic Fiction	
Science Fiction	
Other:	

INGREDIENTS: Write a story summary on the back.
Main Character(s): *Charlotte the spider, Wilbur the pig, Fern the little girl*
Setting: *a farm*

Books Are Good For You

Evaluating books was never so delicious! Duplicate a supply of the Book Nutrition Label on page 66. Cut out each label and paste it to a large index card. Each time a student reads a new book from your classroom library, have him fill out one of the labels. Instruct him to write a short summary of the story on the back of the index card and then place the completed card inside the book. The next time another student wants to know if a book is interesting, he has only to read his peer's review along with the book jacket's description. Instruct each student to fill out a duplicate label and staple the top edge of it into his scrapbook.

Timeline Through Literature

Take a trip to the past using historical fiction! Select five to ten historical fiction books, and display them—out of chronological order—at a learning center. Instruct each student to come to the center, skim each book to determine its time and setting, and then place the books in the correct chronological order. Have the student record this order in his scrapbook. At the end of the week, reveal the correct order.

Hey, we could write about some kids on a cruise ship!

How about, "It was a dark and stormy night"?

In The Beginning

Students who have difficulty choosing books will be interested to know that they can often tell a lot about a book from reading the first few paragraphs. Illustrate this point by selecting several of the novels listed on the right. Read only the first paragraph or two. Discuss the following questions: "What do we learn about this story from these few lines? What mood has the author set up in his story? What do you want to know after hearing these few lines?" Not only will this exercise get students looking more closely at descriptive writing, but it may also inspire your students to read some new books!

Follow up by brainstorming a set of story characters and a story setting. Instruct each student to imagine the story she could write about these characters. Then have the student write the beginning of her story in her scrapbook. Share these story beginnings and have each student explain how she came to begin the tale that way.

The Dark Is Rising by Susan Cooper
Dragonwings by Laurence Yep
From The Mixed-Up Files Of Mrs. Basil E. Frankweiler by E. L. Konigsburg
A Gathering Of Days by Joan W. Blos
The Indian In The Cupboard by Lynne Reid Banks
Matilda by Roald Dahl
Mr. Popper's Penguins by Florence Atwater and Richard Atwater
The Secret Garden by Frances Hodgson Burnett
Shiloh by Phyllis Reynolds Naylor
Stone Fox by John Gardiner
The Summer Of The Swans by Betsy Byars
Thank You, Jackie Robinson by Barbara Cohen
Tuck Everlasting by Natalie Babbitt
The Westing Game by Ellen Raskin
The Wolves Of Willoughby Chase by Joan Aiken
A Wrinkle In Time by Madeleine L'Engle

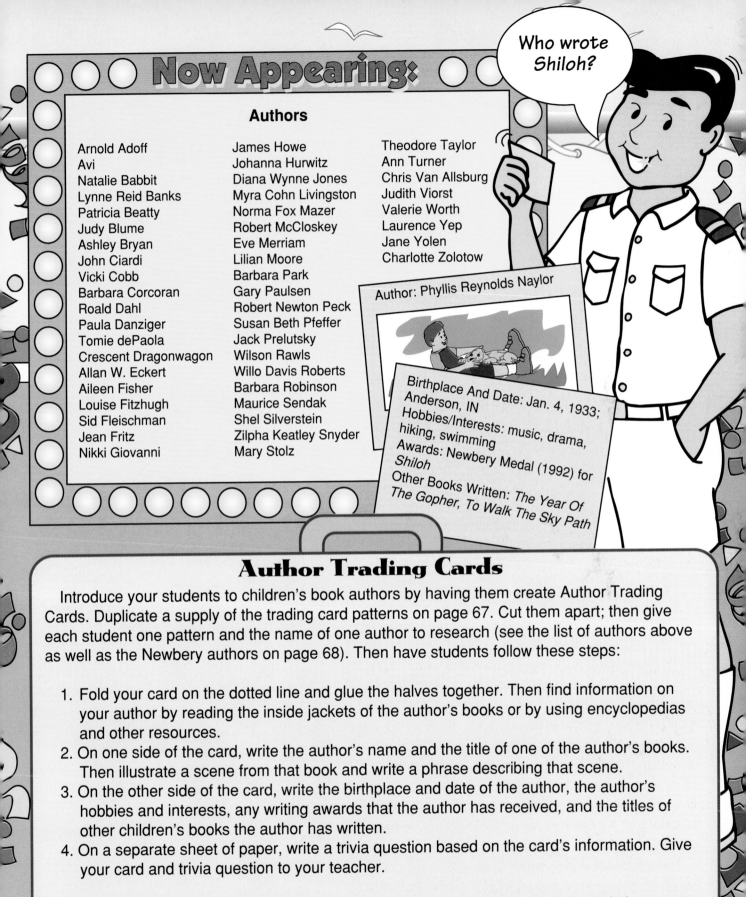

Now Appearing:

Authors

Arnold Adoff
Avi
Natalie Babbit
Lynne Reid Banks
Patricia Beatty
Judy Blume
Ashley Bryan
John Ciardi
Vicki Cobb
Barbara Corcoran
Roald Dahl
Paula Danziger
Tomie dePaola
Crescent Dragonwagon
Allan W. Eckert
Aileen Fisher
Louise Fitzhugh
Sid Fleischman
Jean Fritz
Nikki Giovanni

James Howe
Johanna Hurwitz
Diana Wynne Jones
Myra Cohn Livingston
Norma Fox Mazer
Robert McCloskey
Eve Merriam
Lilian Moore
Barbara Park
Gary Paulsen
Robert Newton Peck
Susan Beth Pfeffer
Jack Prelutsky
Wilson Rawls
Willo Davis Roberts
Barbara Robinson
Maurice Sendak
Shel Silverstein
Zilpha Keatley Snyder
Mary Stolz

Theodore Taylor
Ann Turner
Chris Van Allsburg
Judith Viorst
Valerie Worth
Laurence Yep
Jane Yolen
Charlotte Zolotow

Who wrote Shiloh?

Author: Phyllis Reynolds Naylor

Birthplace And Date: Jan. 4, 1933; Anderson, IN
Hobbies/Interests: music, drama, hiking, swimming
Awards: Newbery Medal (1992) for Shiloh
Other Books Written: The Year Of The Gopher, To Walk The Sky Path

Author Trading Cards

Introduce your students to children's book authors by having them create Author Trading Cards. Duplicate a supply of the trading card patterns on page 67. Cut them apart; then give each student one pattern and the name of one author to research (see the list of authors above as well as the Newbery authors on page 68). Then have students follow these steps:

1. Fold your card on the dotted line and glue the halves together. Then find information on your author by reading the inside jackets of the author's books or by using encyclopedias and other resources.
2. On one side of the card, write the author's name and the title of one of the author's books. Then illustrate a scene from that book and write a phrase describing that scene.
3. On the other side of the card, write the birthplace and date of the author, the author's hobbies and interests, any writing awards that the author has received, and the titles of other children's books the author has written.
4. On a separate sheet of paper, write a trivia question based on the card's information. Give your card and trivia question to your teacher.

Redistribute the cards to the class members; then shuffle the trivia questions and give one to each student. Select one student to ask her question while each of the other students looks at his card to see if it contains the answer. The student who answers correctly gets to ask the next question. Continue playing until all of the questions have been answered.

To Be Or Not To Be... A Student Reader

Harness the dramatic energies of your pupils by having them create story tapes for younger students. Select several outstanding picture books to tape-record. Divide your class into groups of two to four, depending on the number of speaking parts required by the story. Give each group one of the books to read aloud. Encourage students to use dramatic voices and sound effects while reading the book. Then have each group, in turn, record its story on tape. Place each tape with a copy of the book in a large plastic bag; then rotate these book/tape sets among the primary classes for their listening enjoyment. Younger students will be thrilled to hear the big kids speaking, and the primary teachers will appreciate having new selections to use in their listening libraries.

Open Up Your World With Books

Chances are that many of your students have not yet traveled to faraway countries. However, with the growing number of multicultural books, they can learn about different cultures without leaving their desks! Divide your class into six groups. Assign one of the following continents to each group: Europe, North America, South America, Africa, Australia, Asia. Instruct each group to browse in the library to find trade books, folktales, or informational books about countries located within its continent. Next have each group member select a different country from his group's continent and a library book based or set in it. Instruct the student to read his book and complete the postcard pattern on page 66. Then have him flip the card to the blank side and draw a picture that represents something about his book's country.

To display these postcards, enlarge the pattern on page 69 onto poster board. Color and cut it out. Cut the completed world in half; then arrange it on a board as shown. Attach the postcards to the board with pushpins. Invite students to browse through the worldly display of informational book evaluations.

60

Teacher's Choice

What better way to spark interest in reading than to model this skill for your students! Select an appropriate children's book to read while your students are enjoying sustained silent reading. Then make a point each week to give a short presentation on the book you've read. Try a variety of methods when presenting your books. For example, bring in an object that symbolizes one important aspect of the story (an hourglass for *A Wrinkle In Time* or Turkish Delight candy for *The Lion, The Witch, And The Wardrobe*). Or try dressing up as a character, creating a special atmosphere in the room by adjusting the lighting, or playing background music. Always introduce the main characters and the setting, and tell just enough of the plot to whet your students' interest. You may even choose to read a short section of the book—stopping at a crucial point in the story. Not only will you be modeling the joy of reading, but you'll also give students some great ideas for *their* next book reports. Don't be surprised if the book you just read gets checked out immediately!

Author, Author!

Nothing completes a Book Week celebration better than making books to share. Gather a supply of younger children's informational books for your students to study. Point out the small amount of text, the simple sentences, and the arrangement of art on each page. Next assign each of your students one animal to research. Have each student use the library resources to find five interesting, easy-to-understand facts about his animal. Then instruct him to write the facts in short, complete sentences in a logical order. Finally have the student devise a simple question to write at the end of his five statements. The question should be one that encourages the reader to find out more about the animal.

After approving each student's statements and question, choose a bookmaking process to use in creating these informational gems. *A Book Of One's Own: Developing Literacy Through Making Books* by Paul Johnson (Heinemann) and *Making Books Across The Curriculum* by Natalie Walsh (Scholastic Inc.) are two good choices for introducing some creative bookmaking techniques. Once students have completed their books, invite a class of younger students to visit. Pair each younger student with an older one for a time of reading and sharing. If one of the younger students wants to seek more information on the animal, allow your student to accompany her to the media center to find more information.

Newbery Study

Each year since 1922 the American Library Association has awarded the Newbery Medal to the author of a book deemed to make the most outstanding contribution to children's literature. This famous award is named for John Newbery, an 18th-century British bookseller. Have your students read some of these outstanding books (see the list of Newbery winners on page 68). Then have them complete one of the following activities:

- Pair up students. Give each pair two copies of the same Newbery book. After each partner reads the book independently, have him fill out the review reproducible below and paste it into his scrapbook. Then have the two students collaborate to create an informational poster on a 12" x 24" sheet of colored paper. Attach each poster to a coat hanger. Hang the completed posters in the media center or hallway under the title "Hanging Out With The Newbery Winners."

- Pair up students. Give each pair two different Newbery books to read. Have the students read both books and then compare the two stories using Venn diagrams. Instruct the pair to create a separate Venn diagram for characters, setting, plot, and theme. Instruct each student to record the similarities and differences between the two books in his scrapbook.

Maniac Magee by Jerry Spinelli

Plot
Theme
Setting
Characters

- -

Name _____   *Newbery book review*

A Newbery Book: Under Investigation

Title Of Book: _____

Author: _____

Book Summary: _____

_____

_____

Each Newbery Book is selected because of its "outstanding contribution to children's literature." Do you think that this book was a good choice for such a high honor? Explain your answer.

_____

_____

_____

Use this pattern with "Step Aside, Samsonite®!" on page 54 and "Mementos" on page 55.

Patterns

Use with "Step Aside, Samsonite®!" on page 54.

Destination

Activity

Student

Ticket To The Future

Reading definitely takes you to places you have never been! Complete the survey below to discover the types of books that interest you. Then fill out your "Ticket To The Future" with the titles of three interesting books you would like to read. After reading each book, have your teacher stamp the space below the book's title. Bon voyage!

Reading Survey

Complete the statements below. You may check more than one answer.

1. I like to read books that belong to the following group(s):
    - _____ Mystery
    - _____ Science Fiction
    - _____ Humor
    - _____ Historical Fiction
    - _____ Informational
    - _____ Biographical
    - _____ Poetry
    - _____ Fantasy
    - _____ Other: _____

2. I like books in which the main characters are:
    - _____ Girls
    - _____ Boys
    - _____ Animals
    - _____ Adults
    - _____ Other: _____

3. I like to read books that are:
    - _____ Really long
    - _____ Short
    - _____ Collections of short stories

4. Hobbies and/or interests of mine are _____
    _____

5. My favorite book is _____
    I like this book because _____
    _____

Ticket To The Future Admit One _____ Student Name	TITLE	TITLE	TITLE
	STAMP	STAMP	STAMP

©1996 The Education Center, Inc. • *NOVEMBER* • TEC200

Patterns

Use the Book Nutrition Label with "Books Are Good For You" on page 57. Use the postcard pattern with "Open Up Your World With Books" on page 60.

Novel Nutrition Facts

Title: _____

Author: _____

Rating (1–10: 1 = "poor," 10 = "fantastic"): _____

Reasons For Rating: _____

Amount Per Book   % Value

Fantasy _____

Historical Fiction _____

Humor _____

Mystery _____

Realistic Fiction _____

Science Fiction _____

Other: _____

INGREDIENTS: Write a story summary on the back.

Main Character(s): _____

Setting: _____

Dear _____,

    If you want to learn more about

_____, then you
(Name Of Country)

need to read _____
(Title Of Book)

by _____.
(Name Of Author)

From this book I learned _____

_____

_____

_____

_____.

      Yours truly,

_____

The illustrations: _____

To: _____

Book Title: _____

_____

Author: _____

Publisher: _____

Copyright Date: _____

Author: _____

Title: _____
Scene: _____

©1996 The Education Center, Inc.

_____
_____
_____

Other Books Written:

Awards:

Hobbies/Interests:

Birthplace And Date:

Author: _____

Title: _____
Scene: _____

©1996 The Education Center, Inc.

_____
_____
_____

Other Books Written:

Awards:

Hobbies/Interests:

Birthplace And Date:

Author: _____

Title: _____
Scene: _____

©1996 The Education Center, Inc.

_____
_____
_____

Other Books Written:

Awards:

Hobbies/Interests:

Birthplace And Date:

Author: _____

Title: _____
Scene: _____

©1996 The Education Center, Inc.

_____
_____
_____

Other Books Written:

Awards:

Hobbies/Interests:

Birthplace And Date:

John Newbery Award Winners

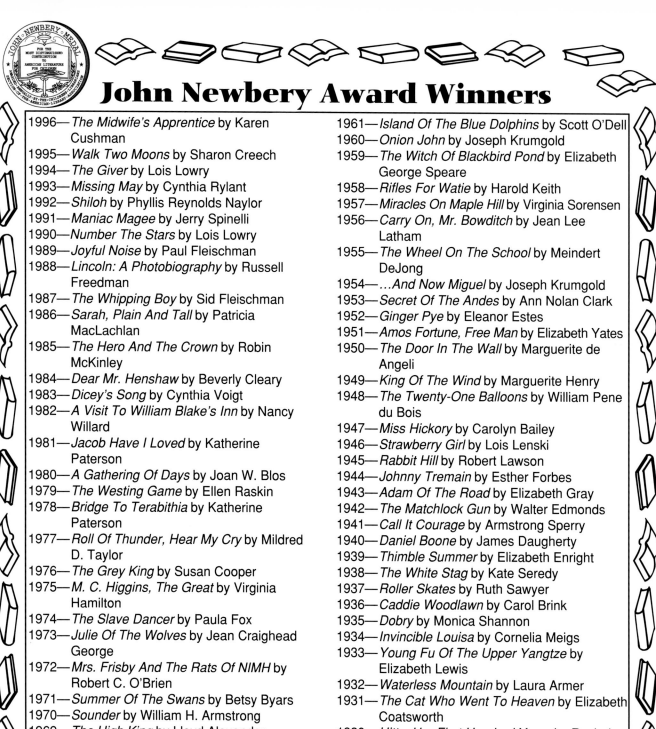

1996— *The Midwife's Apprentice* by Karen Cushman

1995— *Walk Two Moons* by Sharon Creech

1994— *The Giver* by Lois Lowry

1993— *Missing May* by Cynthia Rylant

1992— *Shiloh* by Phyllis Reynolds Naylor

1991— *Maniac Magee* by Jerry Spinelli

1990— *Number The Stars* by Lois Lowry

1989— *Joyful Noise* by Paul Fleischman

1988— *Lincoln: A Photobiography* by Russell Freedman

1987— *The Whipping Boy* by Sid Fleischman

1986— *Sarah, Plain And Tall* by Patricia MacLachlan

1985— *The Hero And The Crown* by Robin McKinley

1984— *Dear Mr. Henshaw* by Beverly Cleary

1983— *Dicey's Song* by Cynthia Voigt

1982— *A Visit To William Blake's Inn* by Nancy Willard

1981— *Jacob Have I Loved* by Katherine Paterson

1980— *A Gathering Of Days* by Joan W. Blos

1979— *The Westing Game* by Ellen Raskin

1978— *Bridge To Terabithia* by Katherine Paterson

1977— *Roll Of Thunder, Hear My Cry* by Mildred D. Taylor

1976— *The Grey King* by Susan Cooper

1975— *M. C. Higgins, The Great* by Virginia Hamilton

1974— *The Slave Dancer* by Paula Fox

1973— *Julie Of The Wolves* by Jean Craighead George

1972— *Mrs. Frisby And The Rats Of NIMH* by Robert C. O'Brien

1971— *Summer Of The Swans* by Betsy Byars

1970— *Sounder* by William H. Armstrong

1969— *The High King* by Lloyd Alexander

1968— *From The Mixed-Up Files Of Mrs. Basil E. Frankweiler* by E. L. Konigsburg

1967— *Up A Road Slowly* by Irene Hunt

1966— *I, Juan de Pareja* by Elizabeth Borten de Treviño

1965— *Shadow Of A Bull* by Maia Wojciechowska

1964— *It's Like This, Cat* by Emily Neville

1963— *A Wrinkle In Time* by Madeleine L'Engle

1962— *The Bronze Bow* by Elizabeth George Speare

1961— *Island Of The Blue Dolphins* by Scott O'Dell

1960— *Onion John* by Joseph Krumgold

1959— *The Witch Of Blackbird Pond* by Elizabeth George Speare

1958— *Rifles For Watie* by Harold Keith

1957— *Miracles On Maple Hill* by Virginia Sorensen

1956— *Carry On, Mr. Bowditch* by Jean Lee Latham

1955— *The Wheel On The School* by Meindert DeJong

1954— *...And Now Miguel* by Joseph Krumgold

1953— *Secret Of The Andes* by Ann Nolan Clark

1952— *Ginger Pye* by Eleanor Estes

1951— *Amos Fortune, Free Man* by Elizabeth Yates

1950— *The Door In The Wall* by Marguerite de Angeli

1949— *King Of The Wind* by Marguerite Henry

1948— *The Twenty-One Balloons* by William Pene du Bois

1947— *Miss Hickory* by Carolyn Bailey

1946— *Strawberry Girl* by Lois Lenski

1945— *Rabbit Hill* by Robert Lawson

1944— *Johnny Tremain* by Esther Forbes

1943— *Adam Of The Road* by Elizabeth Gray

1942— *The Matchlock Gun* by Walter Edmonds

1941— *Call It Courage* by Armstrong Sperry

1940— *Daniel Boone* by James Daugherty

1939— *Thimble Summer* by Elizabeth Enright

1938— *The White Stag* by Kate Seredy

1937— *Roller Skates* by Ruth Sawyer

1936— *Caddie Woodlawn* by Carol Brink

1935— *Dobry* by Monica Shannon

1934— *Invincible Louisa* by Cornelia Meigs

1933— *Young Fu Of The Upper Yangtze* by Elizabeth Lewis

1932— *Waterless Mountain* by Laura Armer

1931— *The Cat Who Went To Heaven* by Elizabeth Coatsworth

1930— *Hitty, Her First Hundred Years* by Rachel Field

1929— *Trumpeter Of Krakow* by Eric P. Kelly

1928— *Gay Neck, The Story Of A Pigeon* by Dhan Mukerji

1927— *Smoky, The Cowhorse* by Will James

1926— *Shen Of The Sea* by Arthur Chrisman

1925— *Tales From Silver Lands* by Charles Finger

1924— *The Dark Frigate* by Charles Hawes

1923— *The Voyages Of Doctor Dolittle* by Hugh Lofting

1922— *The Story Of Mankind* by Henrik Van Loon

©1996 The Education Center, Inc. • *NOVEMBER* • TEC200

Note To The Teacher: Use this page with "Author Trading Cards" on page 59 and "Newbery Study" on page 62.

UP, UP, AND AWAY!

High-Flying Activities For Studying Flight And Aviation

Make your reservations now to investigate the world of flight and aviation with this collection of high-flying, creative activities. Whether you use these ideas to celebrate Aviation History Month in November or add them to your science lesson plans, excitement is sure to soar as students explore the wild blue yonder!

by Lynn Tutterow

100 Years From Now

How many of your students have ever flown in an airplane? Survey the class to find out about their experiences, such as how they felt the first time they flew, their thoughts during takeoff and landing, the size of the plane, and the service offered by the flight attendants. Point out that while we now take flying for granted, 100 years ago it was still a dream. Conclude the discussion by asking students to make predictions about things that people will be able to do 100 years from now that they aren't able to do today. Have students write about their predictions in their journals.

Flying Through Time

As they soar into aviation history, invite your students to make a quick landing at this timely learning center. Duplicate two copies of page 75. Mount one copy on red paper; then glue it to a poster as shown. Enhance the poster with a copy of the plane pattern on page 77. Put a stack of index cards and a supply of paper clips in a pocket attached to the poster. Display the poster at a center. Cut the other list apart; then glue each box onto a separate envelope. Place these envelopes in a basket at the center. Add several aviation history resources to the center. Instruct students to do the following when they visit the center:

1. Select a date/event to research from the list. Write the description of the event at the top of an index card.
2. After researching the event, write three questions about it on the front of the card.
3. On the back of the card, write the name(s) and page number(s) of the reference(s) you used to develop each question.
4. On a separate index card, write the name of the event and the answer to each question.
5. Paper–clip the two index cards together and place them into the matching envelope.

Store these completed card sets at the center in another basket. Encourage students to visit the center and quiz each other on the aviation facts in preparation for the "Flying Facts" game on page 71.

Flying Facts

Combine fact with fun in this high-flying quiz game. Divide the class into teams of six; then number the group members one through six. Give each student a sheet of 8 1/2" x 11" paper. Instruct the student to fold the sheet into a paper airplane; then have him label it with his name.

To play, draw a card from the "Flying Through Time" activity on page 70. Read its date and fact; then read one of the card's questions. Instruct each of the number 1 students to write his answer on a scrap of paper. Check the answers. Give one point to each group whose member answered correctly. Then invite the students who answered correctly to stand at a designated spot on the floor and try to fly their paper airplanes into the trash can or hit some other target. Reward each successful student by giving his team another point. Continue play with the number 2 students and so on until every group member has had a chance to play. Tally the points and applaud the winning team.

1962 John Glenn becomes first American to orbit Earth.

1. With whom did John Glenn travel in his orbit of Earth?
2. What was the name of his spacecraft?
3. How long did it take him to make one orbit of Earth?

Soaring Toward Success

Show off your squadron of hardworking students with this easy-to-make bulletin-board display. Duplicate the hot-air balloon pattern on page 77 for each student. Have each child write her name on the balloon's basket, and then decorate the balloon with markers or crayons. Duplicate the contract on page 76 for each child. For each activity a student completes, place a colorful star sticker on her balloon. When the entire class completes a certain number of activities, treat students to a special "flying saucer" (pizza) lunch!

SOARING TOWARD SUCCESS!

Alex · Juan · James · Teri · Kim · Jan · Chris · Marie · Tim · Anna

Detecting Air Currents

Air travel is made possible by understanding and harnessing the movement of air. Pilots depend on wind gauges to tell them the speed and direction of the wind. Build your own simple wind gauge using a feather, glue, a thimble, a round-top pin, thin wire or string, modeling clay, and a small block of wood.

Glue the feather to the top of the thimble as shown. Allow one to two inches of the shaft to extend on one side. Use modeling clay to attach the pin, with its head facing up, to the block of wood. Place the thimble on top of the pin's head. Wrap thin wire or string around the shaft of the feather until it balances perfectly on the pinhead.

Describe how the air detector behaves when a person walks by, when a door in the room opens and closes, and when everything in the room is "still." Because air is in constant motion, students will observe the air movement detector responding to the slightest movement in the air.

The Montgolfier Brothers' Balloons

In 1783, the Montgolfier brothers from France began experimenting with filling paper and fabric bags with smoke and hot air. In September of that year, they launched a balloon carrying a sheep, a duck, and a rooster. In November, two humans stayed aloft for 25 minutes. The age of flight had begun!

Conduct the following experiment for your students to demonstrate the principles of flight discovered by the Montgolfier brothers.

Materials: a plastic liter bottle, a balloon, a bowl, boiling water, ice (or very cold water), oven mitts

Question: Why does a hot-air balloon float?

Procedure: Place the open end of a balloon over the mouth of the bottle. Stand the bottle in the bowl. While wearing the oven mitts, fill the bowl with boiling water. Record your results. Now pour the hot water out and fill the bowl with ice (or very cold water).

Observations: When the bowl is filled with boiling water, the balloon will inflate. When the bowl is filled with ice, the balloon will deflate.

Conclusions: Hot air molecules occupy a large amount of space in the balloon when they are heated up. It takes fewer heated molecules to fill the balloon. Because there are fewer molecules in the balloon, the balloon becomes light and rises. When the molecules are cooled, they "huddle" together. Therefore, you can fit more of them into the balloon, making it heavy and causing it to sink.

We can visit other countries.

We can bring food to the poor in Bosnia.

Teams can travel to other countries.

We're always a day's travel to anywhere.

The Sky's The Limit!

The Wright brothers' first airplane flight received very little attention because people simply did not believe it was possible for man to fly. However, when Amos Root witnessed the Wrights' plane circling in the air he said, "When Columbus discovered America, he did not know what the outcome would be, and no one at that time knew....In a like manner these two brothers have probably not even a faint glimpse of what their discovery is going to bring to the children of men."

Read this quote to your students. Then ask them, "What has the Wright brothers' discovery brought to you and me—the 'children of men'?" After some discussion, divide your class into small groups. Give each group a different section of a newspaper. Instruct each group to scan the newspaper and cut out three to five articles or advertisements that provide examples of how man's ability to fly has changed our world. Have each group mount each of its articles on a sheet of colored paper, adding a caption that describes how the influence of air travel can be seen in the article. Enlarge, color, and cut out the biplane pattern on page 77; then mount it on a long bulletin board or wall space. Arrange the mounted articles on a banner trailing the plane as shown.

Lifting Off With Literature

Searching the friendly skies for some reference books your students can use as they study aviation? Look no further than these excellent titles:

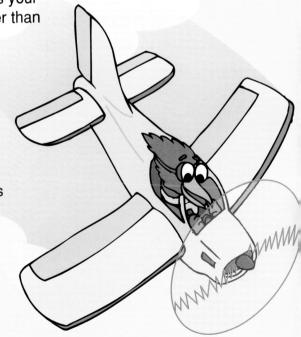

Super Paper Airplanes: Biplanes To Space Planes
written by Norman Schmidt; published by Sterling Publishing Company, Inc.

Airplanes (part of the What If... series)
written by Steve Parker; published by The Millbrook Press

Eureka! It's An Airplane! (part of the Inventing series)
written by Jeanne Bendick; published by The Millbrook Press

Flight
created by Andrew Haslam and written by Jack Challoner; published by Thomson Learning

The Wright Brothers: How They Invented The Airplane
written by Russell Freedman; published by Scholastic Inc.

Black Eagles: African American Aviation
written by Jim Haskins; published by Scholastic Inc.

Lift Off!

Understanding the properties of air enabled the Wright brothers to build the first successful plane. In a specially built wind tunnel, they tested the effect of air on different wing shapes. They discovered that a curved wing produced maximum *lift.* Lift is the upward pull you feel when you place your arm outside a car window while traveling along. Lift in an airplane is produced by differences in air pressure between the air flowing over the curved top of a wing and the air flowing underneath. Air traveling over the curved top of a wing must speed up in order to catch up with the air traveling under the wing. This creates an area of low pressure above the wing causing it to be sucked up into the air. Demonstrate this concept by having each student make the following model:

Materials: ruler, 5" x 1 1/2" strip of paper, tape

Question: How does the shape of a wing affect lift?

Procedure: Fold the strip of paper in half and tape the top edge about 1 1/4" from the bottom edge. This will make the top surface curved and give the paper the shape of an airplane wing (see the illustration below). Slide the ruler into the fold of the paper. Blow on the front of the wing.

Observations: As the student blows on the loop, the taped end rises into the air.

Results: Because the top surface of the wing is curved, the air has to travel a greater distance over the top of the wing than under the bottom of the wing. This creates a difference in air pressure. Since there is more pressure on the bottom of the wing than on the top, the wing is pushed upward.

The Olympics Of Loopy-Loops

Give your students the opportunity to experiment with the principles of air and flight by creating their own paper flying toys. Duplicate page 78 for each student. Instruct each student to follow the directions to create an unusual paper airplane. Then pair students and have them conduct the experiment, noting their observations on the reproducible.

Build on your students' enthusiasm by holding a High-Flying Olympic Competition. Using such books as E. Richard Churchill's *Fantastic Flying Paper Toys* (Sterling Publishing Co., Inc.) and some of those listed on page 73, have each student create a different flying toy. Then hold test flights to see which creation flies the farthest.

Red-Letter Dates In Aviation

Year	Event	Year	Event
1903	Wright brothers complete first engine-powered, heavier-than-air flight.	1954	The Boeing 707, the first large passenger jet, is introduced in U.S.
1907	Glenn H. Curtiss starts first airplane-manufacturing company in America.	1957	Soviet Union launches first artificial satellite, *Sputnik 1.*
1911	Calbraith Rodgers makes first flight across the U.S. in the *Vin Fiz.*	1958	National Aeronautics and Space Administration (NASA) is founded.
1918	U.S. government starts using planes for airmail service.	1958	Congress establishes the Federal Aviation Agency (FAA) to deal with air safety and air traffic control.
1926	Richard E. Byrd and Floyd Bennett make first airplane flight over North Pole.	1959	First commercial airline jet service in U.S. begins.
1927	Charles Lindbergh makes first solo, nonstop flight across Atlantic Ocean.	1961	Alan Shepard, Jr., becomes first American in space.
1932	Amelia Earhart becomes first woman to fly solo, nonstop, across Atlantic Ocean; also flies solo across U.S.	1962	John Glenn becomes first American to orbit Earth.
1933	Wiley Post makes first solo, around-the-world flight in the *Winnie Mae.*	1965	Edward White becomes first American to walk in space.
1939	Igor I. Sikorsky makes first flight of practical single-rotor helicopter in U.S.	1968	*Apollo 8*—manned by Frank Borman; James Lovell, Jr.; and William Anders—orbits moon ten times.
1939	Germany uses its air force, the *Luftwaffe,* to attack Poland; World War II begins.	1981	Space shuttle *Columbia* makes first flight.
1944	Allied forces invade Europe, relying heavily on B-17 Flying Fortress.	1983	Sally Ride becomes first American woman in space.
1945	B-29 *Enola Gay* ends World War II by dropping atomic bomb on Hiroshima, Japan.	1986	Dick Rutan and Jeana Yeager make first nonstop flight around world without refueling.
1947	Charles Yeager makes first flight to break sound barrier.	1990	*Hubble Space Telescope* is launched.

©1996 The Education Center, Inc. • *NOVEMBER* • TEC200

Note To The Teacher: Use this page with "Flying Through Time" on page 70.

Name _____ *Contract*

Soaring Toward Success!

Complete _____ of the activities below by

_____.

(date)

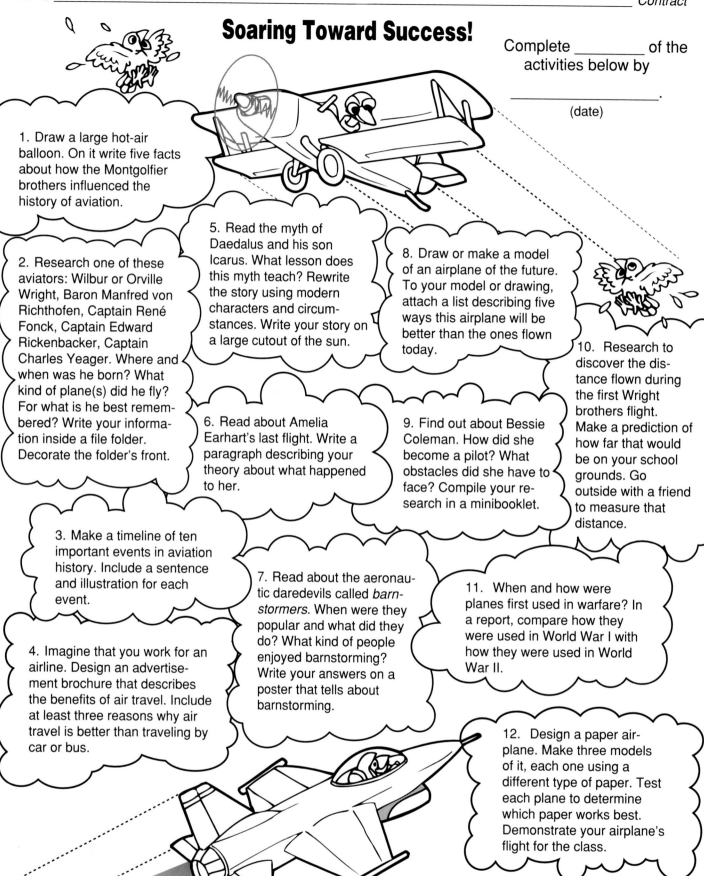

1. Draw a large hot-air balloon. On it write five facts about how the Montgolfier brothers influenced the history of aviation.

2. Research one of these aviators: Wilbur or Orville Wright, Baron Manfred von Richthofen, Captain René Fonck, Captain Edward Rickenbacker, Captain Charles Yeager. Where and when was he born? What kind of plane(s) did he fly? For what is he best remembered? Write your information inside a file folder. Decorate the folder's front.

3. Make a timeline of ten important events in aviation history. Include a sentence and illustration for each event.

4. Imagine that you work for an airline. Design an advertisement brochure that describes the benefits of air travel. Include at least three reasons why air travel is better than traveling by car or bus.

5. Read the myth of Daedalus and his son Icarus. What lesson does this myth teach? Rewrite the story using modern characters and circumstances. Write your story on a large cutout of the sun.

6. Read about Amelia Earhart's last flight. Write a paragraph describing your theory about what happened to her.

7. Read about the aeronautic daredevils called *barnstormers*. When were they popular and what did they do? What kind of people enjoyed barnstorming? Write your answers on a poster that tells about barnstorming.

8. Draw or make a model of an airplane of the future. To your model or drawing, attach a list describing five ways this airplane will be better than the ones flown today.

9. Find out about Bessie Coleman. How did she become a pilot? What obstacles did she have to face? Compile your research in a minibooklet.

10. Research to discover the distance flown during the first Wright brothers flight. Make a prediction of how far that would be on your school grounds. Go outside with a friend to measure that distance.

11. When and how were planes first used in warfare? In a report, compare how they were used in World War I with how they were used in World War II.

12. Design a paper airplane. Make three models of it, each one using a different type of paper. Test each plane to determine which paper works best. Demonstrate your airplane's flight for the class.

Note To The Teacher: Use this page with the "Soaring Toward Success" bulletin board on page 71. Write the required number of activities and the due date in the blanks before duplicating. Have each student staple his copy of this page inside a folder; then have him store his work inside the folder.

Patterns

Use with "Soaring Toward Success" on page 71.

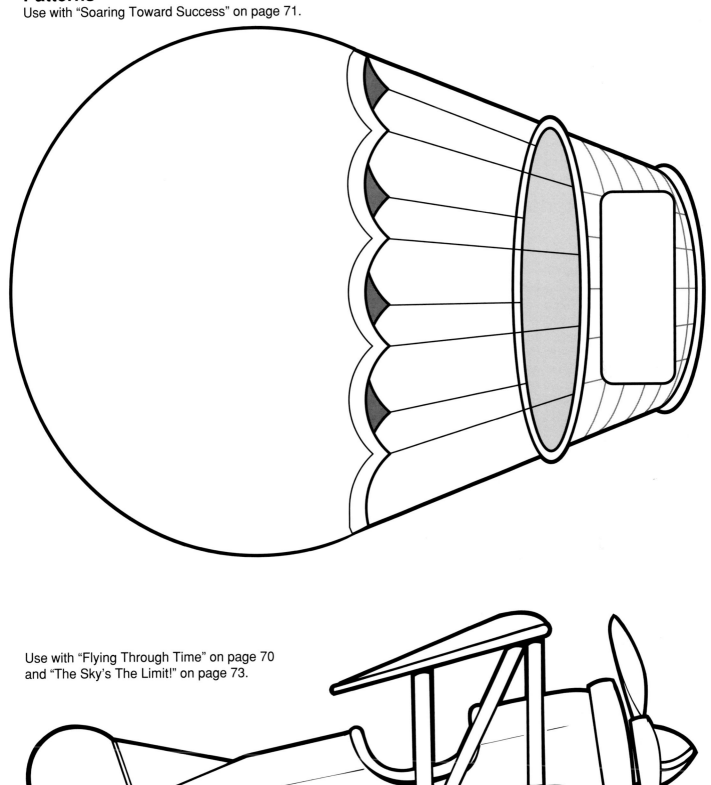

Use with "Flying Through Time" on page 70
and "The Sky's The Limit!" on page 73.

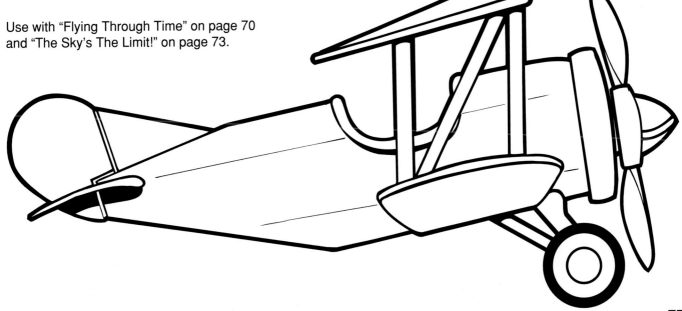

Flight Of The Loopy-Loop

Complete the following directions to create an unusual paper airplane. Then test the flying ability of your creation.

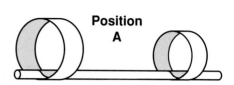

Throw

Position A

Materials: 8" drinking straw, tape, 3/4" x 6 1/2" strip of paper, 1" x 7" strip of paper, a measuring tape for each pair of students

Position B

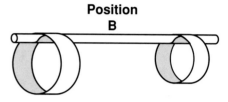

Directions For Making A Plane: Loop each paper strip by overlapping the ends just enough to form a pocket for holding the straw; then tape the ends together. (One loop should be larger than the other loop.) Slide one end of the straw into the pocket of the larger loop. Slide the other end of the straw into the pocket of the smaller loop.

Position C

Loops three inches apart and equal distances from the ends of the straw

Flight Instructions:

1. Pair up with a friend. Mark a throwing point on the floor with tape. You will start each trial flight from this point.
2. Position one of your planes according to diagram A; then throw it. (Always throw with the small loop in the front of the plane. Also, use the same arm for every throw.) Measure the distance with the measuring tape and record it in the chart below. Then throw the plane two more times in this position. Measure; then record the distance and your observations in the chart.
3. Repeat step 2 for positions B–D. Be sure to use the same throwing arm that you used for position A.
4. Repeat steps 2–3 with your partner's plane.

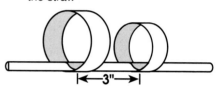

|←—3"—→|

Position D

Same as C, but with loops down

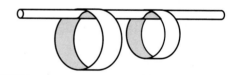

Positions	Distance Flown			Observations
	Flight #1	Flight #2	Flight #3	
A. Loops Up				
B. Loops Down				
C. Loops Up, 3" Apart				
D. Loops Down, 3" Apart				

Find the average distance flown by your plane for each position.

Position A _____   Position C _____

Position B _____   Position D _____

In which position did the plane fly the farthest? _____

Bonus Box: Predict how well the plane would fly with the large loop facing the front. Test your prediction by repeating the above experiment with the plane in that position.

Leaving On A Jet Plane

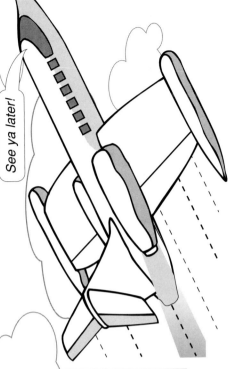

See ya later!

Use the following table to answer the questions below:

	Learjet 35A	Sailplane/Glider	World War I Biplane
Passenger Seats	8	2	1
Length	48 ft. 8 in.	26 ft. 9 in.	18 ft. 9 in.
Height	12 ft. 3 in.	9 ft.	9 ft.
Wingspan	39 ft. 6 in.	57 ft.	28 ft.
Empty Weight	9,838 lb.	831 lb.	950 lb.
Maximum Speed	.81 Mach*	150 mph	112.7 mph

* *Mach:* a high speed expressed by a Mach number. Mach 1 is the speed of sound, or 1,116 feet per second. The Learjet can travel at almost the speed of sound.

1. Which plane is the lightest? _____
   The fastest? _____

2. How much larger is the wingspan of the sailplane than the wingspan of the biplane? _____

3. How much faster can a sailplane travel than a biplane? _____

4. Look up *glider* in the dictionary. How is a glider very different from the other two planes? _____

5. Rank the three planes in order (from least to greatest) according to how much fuel they use. _____

   Explain your reasons for ranking the planes in this order. _____

6. Which plane would be the most useful if you and your family had to get someplace quickly? _____
   Explain your reasons for not choosing the other two planes. _____

7. Which plane would have the quietest ride? _____
   Why? _____

8. The Learjet 35A is the heaviest of the planes and can travel the fastest. What conclusions can you draw from this information? _____

Bonus Box: Describe or draw an aircraft of your own design on the back of this page. Then make a table listing the vital information about your aircraft.

Note To The Teacher: Each student will need access to a dictionary to complete this activity.

The Road To The White House

Activities To Teach The Election Process

The countdown toward Election Day is filled with excitement and anticipation, whether it's a race for the presidency or for a seat on the city council. Give your students insight into the political processes that make it all happen with these terrific thematic activities!

by Paula Holdren

Send Me To The White House!

Plunge into the election frenzy by holding a mock classroom election, timed to coincide with Election Day! Simply follow this day-by-day plan to take your class down a campaign trail that's both fun and educational.

Day 1:
- Ask each student interested in announcing his candidacy for class president to write a letter that declares his desire and lists his qualifications.
- Have each student share his letter with the class. Then narrow the field of candidates to three by having a primary election (class vote).
- Next have the class vote to decide whether the focus of the campaign will be school issues *(more lunchroom choices, better variety of school-store items, more playground or gym equipment, etc.)* OR national issues *(taxes, crime, education, the environment, etc.).*
- Direct each candidate to take a position on the chosen issues.

Days 2–3:
- Have each candidate study the issues (to prepare for an upcoming debate), write a campaign slogan for her committee to use, and write an acceptance speech. Also have the candidate write a congratulatory speech so she'll be ready for whatever outcome the election brings.
- Divide the rest of the class into three groups:
  - *Campaign Committee (for each candidate):* promotes its candidate by making posters and buttons.
  - *Election Committee:* registers voters by gathering class members' signatures on a list; makes a ballot and ballot box; counts the ballots.
  - *Media Committee:* makes a box for collecting class members' questions for candidates to answer during a debate on the issues; also interviews the candidates and writes profiles so class members can study them before they vote.
- Allow time for the groups to meet, plan, and carry out their work.

Day 4:
- Have the candidates debate the issues by answering the questions submitted by class members and collected by media committee members.
- Direct the media committee to distribute candidates' profiles to class members.

Day 5: Election Day
- Allow registered voters to cast their ballots.
- Announce the winner, give time for opponents to make congratulatory speeches, and then have the winner make his acceptance speech.
- Celebrate with punch and sugar cookies (decorated with red, white, and blue frosting) while the class watches the early election coverage on TV.

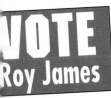

Politically Speaking...

Help your students pick up a little political jargon by making vocabulary placards to display the new terms they learn. Give each student a 4" x 6" index card, a 5" x 7" sheet of red construction paper, a 1" x 6" strip of blue construction paper, a fine-tipped blue marker, glue, and a dictionary. Assign each student a term from the list below. Using the blue marker, have the student print his word and its definition on the index card. Tell the student to glue the index card to the red paper and then glue on the blue strip as a placard "post." Display the placards on a bulletin board titled "Election-Year Jargon."

poll:
the place where voting is done

ballot
campaign
candidate
caucus
convention
debate
delegate
democracy

democratic
Election Day
elector
electoral college
mascot
nominate
party
platform

political
politician
politics
poll
primary
propaganda
recount

referendum
register
republican
slogan
ticket
vote
write-in

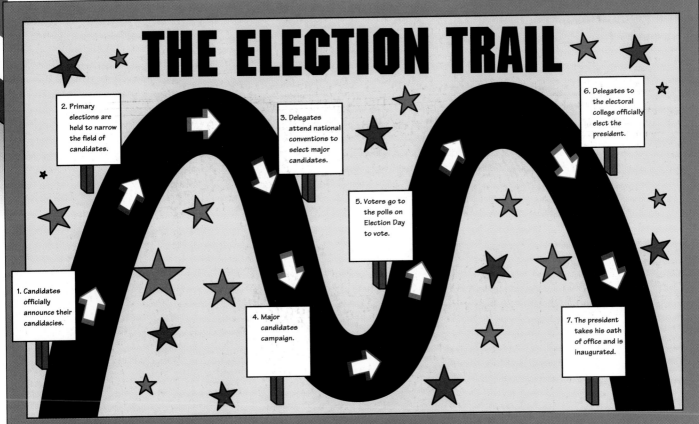

THE ELECTION TRAIL

1. Candidates officially announce their candidacies.

2. Primary elections are held to narrow the field of candidates.

3. Delegates attend national conventions to select major candidates.

4. Major candidates campaign.

5. Voters go to the polls on Election Day to vote.

6. Delegates to the electoral college officially elect the president.

7. The president takes his oath of office and is inaugurated.

Going With The Flow

Getting a president elected involves a lot of hard work long before Election Day. Help your students understand this process by making a class flowchart. On one large piece of paper, copy step 1 from the bulletin board. Then divide your class into six groups and give each group its own sheet of paper. Assign each group one of the remaining steps (2 through 7) shown on the bulletin board. Direct the group to research its step and illustrate it on the paper. Have one of the groups also illustrate step 1, which you labeled earlier. Arrange the steps as signs along a road that you've drawn on a bulletin board titled "The Election Trail." Use arrows as lane dividers to show the sequence of events that leads to the Capitol Hill inauguration.

Voting—A Constitutional Right

Election Day is a day of choices. Voters not only select candidates for office, but they also decide whether to vote at all. In our country, voting is voluntary and the responsibility to carry out this privilege rests privately with each individual. In every election, significant numbers of voters still stay away from the polls. Use the activities on this page to help students understand more about this special privilege.

The People's Choice

Brainstorm with your students creative ways to get larger numbers of people to vote. *(Possible solutions range from making voting mandatory to changing Election Day to a weekend day to offering to babysit so a parent of a young child can make it to the polls.)* Then turn your students loose with poster board, glitter, red-white-and-blue crepe paper, and other art supplies to create attention-getting posters that will encourage folks to get out and vote. Ask parent volunteers to display these posters in their workplaces.

When Can I Vote?

Help your students appreciate the struggle that different groups endured to win the privilege of voting. Review with students what the 15th Amendment, the women's suffrage movement of the early 1900s, the 1965 Voting Rights Act, and the 26th Amendment did to guarantee voters' rights. Then discuss the ideal voting age. Is 18 the best age? Should the legal voting age be lowered or raised? Why? Divide students into groups of like opinions. Have students write reasons for their opinions and defend them with examples. Then allow these groups to debate each other.

As a great follow-up activity, have students get their parents' views on the appropriate voting age. Show both students' and parents' opinions in a graph. Then have students draw conclusions about any similarities or differences in the data.

Take Me Along

Send your students on an Election Day field trip with their parents! Prior to Election Day, send home a note telling about the class's study of elections. State in the note that you wish for students to accompany their parents to the polls on Election Day. This may require that some parents get up earlier or rearrange their schedules, but most parents will be pleased to have their child come along with them. The next day give each child the form on the top of page 89 and have him describe his trip. Enlarge the party symbols on page 88. Then display the students' descriptions with them on a bulletin board titled "To The Polls And Back!"

Me, too!
And I eve
got to me
one of th
candidate

I went with my parents and watched them vote.

Dear Mr. President

Your youngsters may be too young to vote, but they're not too young to voice their opinions—even to their country's leader! Use this letter-writing activity to spark critical thinking about national and foreign-policy issues. Borrow several daily newspapers from your media center. Distribute only sections that deal with national or foreign-policy issues to pairs of students. Direct the students to browse through the sections and categorize relevant topics on paper under two headings: "National" or "Foreign Policy." Have each student choose the topic that most interests him and write a letter expressing his opinion to the president of the United States. Mail the letters to the address shown.

You can also send a class letter to the president via the Internet at president@whitehouse.gov. If you prefer, first browse the White House's Web site at http://wwwwhitehouse.gov.

president@whitehouse.gov.
http://wwwwhitehouse.gov.

Welcome To The White House!

Stacey Andrews
1500 Indiana Court
Jackson, MS 49321

The President of the United States
White House Office
1600 Pennsylvania Avenue NW
Washington, DC 20500

Help At Your Fingertips

If you know where to turn, you can capitalize on a wealth of election information that's available to teachers at little or no cost! Try these helpful suggestions:

- Contact your local chapter of the League of Women Voters for profiles on the candidates and for information on other teaching materials.
- Check with your local newspaper to determine if it plans to publish a special edition of election materials for students. Also ask for information on local races.
- Ask your local city/county clerk's office in charge of voter registration to provide your class with sample ballots and information on voter registration.
- Request campaign materials (buttons, bumper stickers, etc.) and information on specific candidates from your local Democratic and Republican Party headquarters.

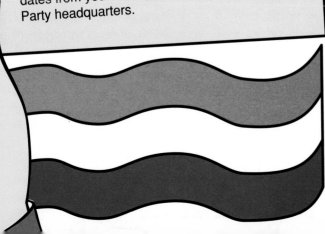

Believe It Or Not

Do you believe *everything* you read about candidates? Of course not! So use election time to help students distinguish between campaign fact and campaign fiction. Start by describing some of the propaganda techniques used by candidates during a campaign:

Bandwagon: This technique tries to persuade everyone to join in and do the same thing, to jump on the bandwagon, and vote for the same candidate.
Testimonial: An important person or a famous figure endorses a candidate.
Name-calling: Negative words are used to create an unfavorable opinion of the other candidate.
Repetition: A candidate's name, or a key phrase representing that candidate, is repeated several times; by the end of the speech or advertisement, the candidate's name or what he represents will be remembered.

Divide students into four groups. Assign a different propaganda technique to each group. Give each group a highlighting marker and a supply of newspaper or newsmagazine articles about candidates. Direct each group to highlight and cut out samples of its technique to mount on poster board and share with the class. How does each candidate try to project himself? His opponent? Continue to examine propaganda with the activities on page 84.

83

The Media Challenge

Turn your students into teams of media analysts! Have students compare and contrast TV news reports with printed campaign literature. Videotape segments of the nightly news that report on different candidates' campaigns. Request samples of the candidates' own literature (see "Help At Your Fingertips" on page 83). Then divide students into groups and give each group samples of campaign literature to study. What image of the candidate is being projected? What does each ad tell you specifically about the candidate and his/her stand on major issues?

After the groups have studied the campaign literature, play the videotaped segments of the nightly news. Have each group compare and contrast the news reports with the literature distributed by the candidates; then have students draw conclusions about the media's impact on elections. *(See the next activity for another look at the media's role in the election process.)*

One More Look

After experiencing "The Media Challenge" above, have your expert campaign analysts examine television ads at home! For homework ask students to listen to and time several television ads paid for by candidates or their committees. Have each student use the following questions to conduct an analysis of each ad:

- What type of background music is used in the ad?
- What type of people are shown in the ad?
- What emotions are felt when watching and listening to the ad?
- What time is this ad being telecast? Why this particular time?
- Which candidates have more or longer ads during the viewing time?

The following day have students discuss and compare their analyses. See if any conclusions can be drawn about the primary purposes of the ads—and about the time of day or evening that most of them were aired. Then have each student demonstrate what he's learned about propaganda techniques by writing an original campaign ad for a candidate of his choice.

Guest Speaker

Discover firsthand what it's like to cover an election campaign! Invite a local television reporter to your class to discuss his/her role in the election coverage. Prior to the reporter's visit, brainstorm with your class key questions that students should ask. Is a reporter always assigned to a particular candidate or does she get to choose whom she covers? If a reporter is assigned to a candidate for whom she doesn't personally plan to vote, does that make her job more difficult? Does the reporter ever interview the candidate or does she just summarize what the candidate does and says? Afterward have each student write a personal thank-you note to the reporter for taking time to visit the class.

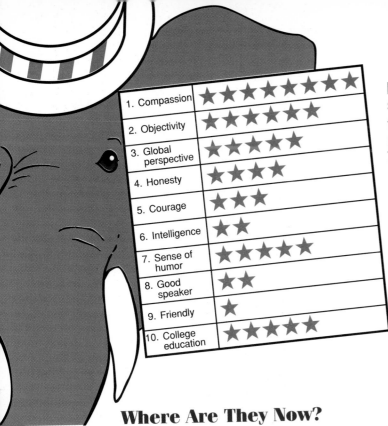

1. Compassion	★★★★★★★★★
2. Objectivity	★★★★★★
3. Global perspective	★★★★★
4. Honesty	★★★★
5. Courage	★★★
6. Intelligence	★★
7. Sense of humor	★★★★★
8. Good speaker	★★
9. Friendly	★
10. College education	★★★★★

Have You Got What It Takes?

Aside from citizenship and age requirements, political candidates must possess certain personal qualities. Have students brainstorm what these must-have attributes are. Honesty? Objectivity? Calmness under pressure? A global perspective? Have the class vote to reduce this list to ten characteristics. Then have each student individually rank each item in the class list in the order of its importance. Tabulate students' opinions for each separate trait. Then divide students into groups to graph the results on posters to share with other classes. As each group delivers its poster, have the students invite the class to produce a Presidential Profile of its own. Then post each class's profile in a hallway for everyone to view and compare.

Where Are They Now?

What happens to presidential candidates who lose their elections—do they *really* lose? Have each student examine the life of an individual who lost a presidential election. Assign each student a name from the list below. Give each student a copy of the reproducible on the bottom of page 89; then have the student research to find out what became of his person. Did he regroup and try again later? Did he disappear from public life altogether? Or did he go on to make significant contributions in another area of service? When students have learned the answers to these questions, have them post them on a chart. Then have the class categorize the answers on the chalkboard under three headings: Ran Again, Left Public Life, Served In Other Areas. Let this lead into a discussion about the lesson that can be learned from examining these candidates' actions—the art of losing gracefully.

Losing Presidential Candidates From 1900 To 1992

William J. Bryan
Alton B. Parker
Theodore Roosevelt
William H. Taft
Charles E. Hughes
James M. Cox
John W. Davis
Alfred E. Smith
Herbert Hoover
Alfred Landon
Wendell Willkie
Thomas E. Dewey
Strom Thurmond
Henry A. Wallace

Adlai E. Stevenson
Richard M. Nixon
Barry M. Goldwater
Hubert H. Humphrey
George C. Wallace
George S. McGovern
Gerald R. Ford
Jimmy Carter
John B. Anderson
Walter F. Mondale
Michael S. Dukakis
George Bush
H. Ross Perot

35¢ **The Daily News** November 5, 1980

Reagan Wins Presidency

Carter loses reelection bid to Ronald Reagan.

Reagan, at 69, is the oldest president ever elected.

Carter only carried 6 states and the District of Columbia for 49 electoral votes.

It Takes Two

Here's a great center idea for learning about the two-party system! Write "Democrat Or Republican?" in block letters on a sheet of white poster board. Enlarge and color the donkey and elephant mascots on page 88; then glue them to the poster. Make two construction-paper pockets. Label one pocket "Take One" and the other "Answer Key." Laminate the pockets for durability and staple them to the poster. Fill the "Take One" pocket with a class supply of the form at the bottom of this page. Duplicate and laminate the answer key for "Democrat Or Republican?" on page 96 and put it in its pocket. Mount the poster at a center. Place encyclopedias, a current almanac, and books like *The Election Book: People Pick A President* by Tamara Hanneman (Scholastic Inc.) and *Our Elections* by Richard Steins (The Millbrook Press) at the center.

Name _____

Democrat Or Republican?

Read each phrase below. Decide whether it describes the Democratic Party or the Republican Party. Use encyclopedias or other resources to help you decide. To show your answer, write a √ or an X in one of the chart's columns next to each phrase. List the name (you'll need to abbreviate) and page number of the resource book you used to find your answer.

★ ★

1. donkey mascot
2. elephant mascot
3. the nation's oldest existing political party
4. historically supported by poor people, factory workers, and minorities
5. known as the "party of prosperity" during the 1920s
6. expanded the role of government beginning about 1913
7. grew out of antislavery meetings
8. formed in 1828 when Andrew Jackson ran for president
9. the Grand Old Party (GOP)
10. usually gets the votes in large cities such as Chicago and New York City
11. usually gets the votes in rural areas
12. President Ronald Reagan's party
13. President Bill Clinton's party
14. President John F. Kennedy's party

Bonus Box: Sometimes a third political party forms. No third-party candidate has ever won the presidency. Yet some people do vote for a third-party candidate, even though his/her chances of winning are not good. Why do you think this is so? Write your answer on the back of this page.

	Democratic Party	Republican Party	Resource Used	Page Number
1.				
2.				
3.				
4.				
5.				
6.				
7.				
8.				
9.				
10.				
11.				
12.				
13.				
14.				

Note To The Teacher: Duplicate a class supply of this form to place in the learning center described in "It Takes Two" at the top of this page.

Name _____ *Critical thinking, problem solving*

Add It Up!

Did you know that in presidential elections in the United States, voters are *really* voting for members of a group called the Electoral College? These persons—called *electors*—promise to vote for the candidate who received the most votes from the people of their states. Candidates with the most *popular votes* (votes from the people) usually receive all of a state's *electoral votes.* The candidate with the most electoral votes wins.

Each state has the same number of electors as it has senators and representatives in Congress. The larger a state's population, the more electors it has.

Study the map. Then use it to help you answer the questions below.

Electoral Votes For President
Based On 1990 Census

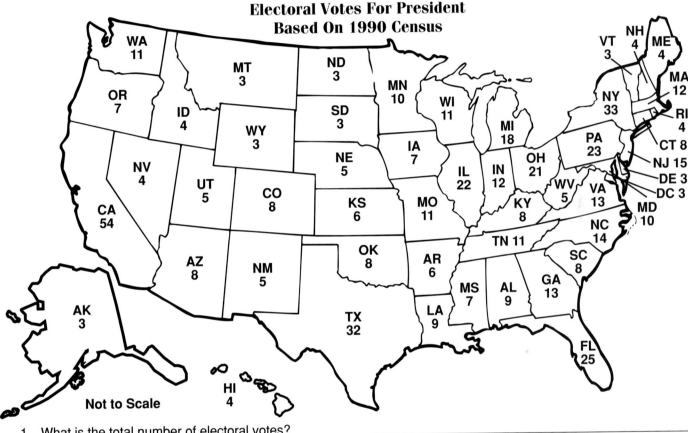

1. What is the total number of electoral votes? _____

2. How many votes does your state have? _____

3. Which four states have the most electoral votes? _____

   _____

4. List at least four states that have just three electoral votes each. _____

   _____

5. If you were a candidate, in which states would you spend most of your time and resources campaigning?

   _____

   Why? _____

6. How many electoral votes does it take to win the presidency? Use a reference book to help you find the answer.

   _____

7. On the back of this page, make a list of states that would give a candidate the number of votes needed to win.

Bonus Box: What happens when there is *no* candidate who receives the number of electoral votes needed to win? Research to find out. Write the answer on the back of this page.

Patterns

Enlarge and use with "Take Me Along" on page 82 and "It Takes Two" on page 86.

©1996 The Education Center, Inc. • *NOVEMBER* • TEC200

A Trip To The Polls

The polling place was _____
_____

I saw _____
_____

Before my parent(s) voted, _____
_____

To vote, my parent(s) _____
_____

I think voting is _____
_____
_____

_____   _____
Date   Name

Where Is _____ Now?
(Name Of Candidate)

Election Of:
_____
(Year)

Lost Election To:
_____
(Name Of Winner)

After the election, this candidate _____
_____
_____
_____
_____
_____

_____
(Name Of Student)

Note To The Teacher: Duplicate one copy of "A Trip To The Polls" for each student to use with "Take Me Along" on page 82. Duplicate one copy of "Where Is ____ Now?" for each student to use with "Where Are They Now?" on page 85.

89

Heroes Of Freedom

Activities For Celebrating Veterans Day

On November 11 we celebrate Veterans Day to honor the former members of the United States Armed Forces. Enlist your students in the following activities to commemorate these heroes of freedom.

by Paula Holdren

Eleventh-Hour Ceremony

Veterans Day was originally called Armistice Day to commemorate the signing of the *armistice,* or truce, that ended World War I. This truce was signed at the eleventh hour of the eleventh day in the eleventh month of 1918. Years later, in 1954, President Dwight D. Eisenhower signed an act of Congress to honor veterans annually on November 11 and to dedicate the day to world peace.

Observe this solemn occasion with your own students on the eleventh hour of the eleventh day of the eleventh month, too. Select from the following activities to design your own 11:00 ceremony for November 11:

- Review the major military conflicts in which our country's armed forces have been involved.
- Recite the Pledge of Allegiance.
- Discuss the characteristics of a hero; then complete the activity on page 94.
- Sing patriotic songs such as "America" or "The Star-Spangled Banner."
- Write letters to the president and Congress urging them to continue to work for world peace.

Home At Last

A soldier who has completed a tour of duty looks forward to returning home. However, returning home means that the soldier must learn to cope with changes in her own life as well as changes that occurred at home while she was away. Have each student brainstorm a list of physical and personal changes that have occurred in her own life in the last six months. For example, the student may have made a new friend, witnessed her parents' divorce, grown a few inches taller, or watched as a new shopping mall was built. Invite willing students to share how they have coped with the changes in their lives. Next brainstorm the changes that a soldier might encounter upon returning home and how he or she could cope with those changes. Then instruct each student to describe in her journal a change a soldier might face and how the soldier could best cope with the change.

Our Defenders Of Freedom

What is it like when a family member serves in the military? Explore this question by reading aloud the picture book *Casey Over There* by Staton Rabin (Harcourt Brace & Company). With simple prose and luminescent illustrations, this story explores the thoughts and feelings of Aubrey, whose brother is a soldier stationed in France during World War I. After discussing the story, have students share experiences in which family members have served as soldiers.

Explore this topic further by inviting former servicemen or women to speak to your class about their military experiences. Help students develop interview questions that ask for general biographical information as well as about how military service has changed their lives. Send each guest speaker a copy of the questions prior to his visit so that he knows which topics to address. Invite the speakers to bring items of interest such as dog tags, uniforms, souvenirs, or medals. Provide a large world map so your guests can point out the countries where they served. Then sit back and enjoy learning about the experiences of these defenders of freedom.

Mr. Mihan's Class Welcomes Our Veterans!

World War II

Fighting Fashion

Today's United States soldier wears a contemporary uniform designed for comfort, durability, and efficiency in modern military situations. However, military uniforms have changed over the years. Increase your students' understanding of history and current events by having them research trends in U.S. military uniforms. First have the class brainstorm a list of military engagements in which the United States has been involved (for example: the Revolutionary War, the War of 1812, the Civil War, the Spanish-American War, World War I, World War II, the Korean War, the Vietnam War, the Gulf War). Give each group of students a four- to five-foot length of white bulletin-board paper. As one group member lies down on the paper, direct the other members to trace an outline of his body.

Next have each group research the uniforms worn by U.S. soldiers during one of the military conflicts listed above. Have the group use crayons, glue, fabric scraps, and construction paper to "dress" its tracing in a uniform worn by soldiers during its assigned war. Instruct the group to write a description of the uniform on an index card secured to the tracing. Display these figures in the hall under the title "American Uniforms Through The Centuries."

Think On These

Take a few moments each day during Veterans Day week to reflect on some of the issues surrounding this special holiday. Write the journal topics at the right on a poster and post it in the classroom. Each day have students select a new topic to write about in their journals.

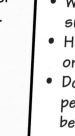

✪ ✪ ✪ Veterans Day Reflections ✪ ✪ ✪

- Have you ever believed in anything so strongly that you were willing to fight or give your life for that belief? If yes, describe what you believed in and why it was so important to you. If no, describe something you might be willing to fight for if necessary.
- What personal qualities best qualify someone for a successful military career?
- How would you feel if your parent, teacher, sibling, or best friend were called to active duty?
- Do you think that the United States should act as peacekeeper for the world? Or do you think it would be better for our country to leave other nations to solve their own problems? Explain.
- Describe how your life might be different if the United States and its allies had lost World War II.

Veterans Day Flap Books

Veterans Day brings to mind the sacrifices that our armed forces have made in service to our country. Use this holiday as the springboard for a unique writing-workshop assignment. As a class, brainstorm a list of ideas to write under each of these headings:

- Why Our Country Needs Armed Forces
- How The Armed Forces Have Helped Our Country
- Sacrifices That Soldiers And Their Families Have Made
- What I Can Learn From A Veteran

Have each student incorporate an item(s) from this list of ideas into an original story about a veteran. Then have the student create a flap book by following the directions below. Share the finished books with a class of primary students.

Directions For Making A Flap Book:
1. Fold a 12" x 18" sheet of white paper in half lengthwise.
2. Using a ruler and pencil, divide the top flap of the paper into three equal segments.
3. Cut along the lines you drew in Step 2 to the fold. Do not cut the fold.
4. Copy your story in the sections under the flaps.
5. On the front of each flap, draw a picture that illustrates the portion of the story written under the flap.